FRANCIS FRITH'S

KIRKCALDY - A HISTORY AND CELEBRATION

THE FRANCIS FRITH COLLECTION

www.francisfrith.com

KIRKCALDY

A HISTORY AND CELEBRATION
OF THE TOWN

KIRKCALDY CIVIC SOCIETY

THE FRANCIS FRITH COLLECTION

www.francisfrith.com

First published in the United Kingdom in 2005
by The Francis Frith Collection®

Hardback edition 2005 ISBN 1-84567-749-8
Paperback edition 2012 ISBN 978-1-84589-702-4

British Library Cataloguing in Publication Data

Kirkcaldy - A History and Celebration of the Town
Kirkcaldy Civic Society

The Francis Frith Collection®
Oakley Business Park, Wylye Road,
Dinton, Wiltshire SP3 5EU
Tel: +44 (0) 1722 716 376
Email: info@francisfrith.co.uk
www.francisfrith.com

Printed and bound in Great Britain
Contains material sourced from responsibly managed forests

Front Cover: **KIRKCALDY, HIGH STREET c1950** KR0001St

All photographs and other illustrative material supplied by Kirkcaldy Civic
Society unless otherwise stated.
Domesday extract used in timeline by kind permission of
Alecto Historical Editions, www.domesdaybook.org
Aerial photographs reproduced under licence from
Simmons Aerofilms Limited.
Historical Ordnance Survey maps reproduced under licence from
Homecheck.co.uk

Every attempt has been made to contact copyright holders of
illustrative material. We will be happy to give full acknowledgement in
future editions for any items not credited. Any information should be
directed to The Francis Frith Collection.

*The colour-tinting in this book is for illustrative purposes only,
and is not intended to be historically accurate*

Contents

KIRKCALDY FROM THE AIR 1966 AFA167441

Historical Timeline for Kirkcaldy

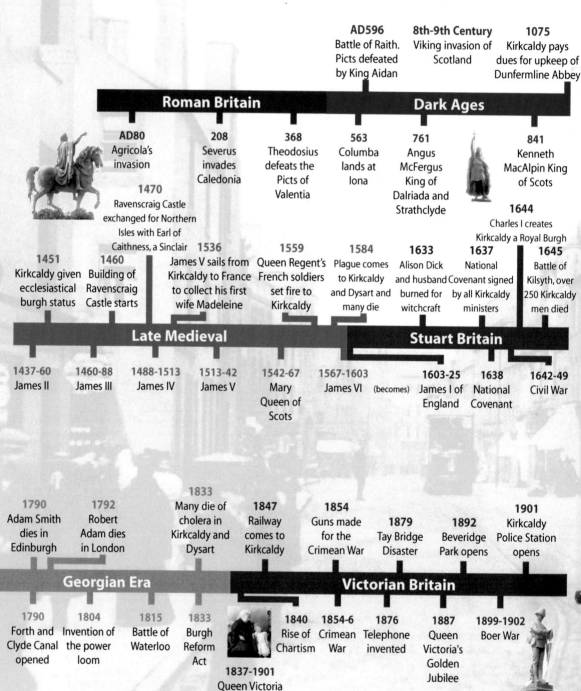

AD596
Battle of Raith.
Picts defeated
by King Aidan

8th-9th Century
Viking invasion of
Scotland

1075
Kirkcaldy pays
dues for upkeep of
Dunfermline Abbey

Roman Britain

Dark Ages

AD80
Agricola's
invasion

208
Severus
invades
Caledonia

368
Theodosius
defeats the
Picts of
Valentia

563
Columba
lands at
Iona

761
Angus
McFergus
King of
Dalriada and
Strathclyde

841
Kenneth
MacAlpin King
of Scots

1470
Ravenscraig Castle
exchanged for Northern
Isles with Earl of
Caithness, a Sinclair

1644
Charles I creates
Kirkcaldy a Royal Burgh

1451
Kirkcaldy given
ecclesiastical
burgh status

1460
Building of
Ravenscraig
Castle starts

1536
James V sails from
Kirkcaldy to France
to collect his first
wife Madeleine

1559
Queen Regent's
French soldiers
set fire to
Kirkcaldy

1584
Plague comes
to Kirkcaldy
and Dysart and
many die

1633
Alison Dick
and husband
burned for
witchcraft

1637
National
Covenant signed
by all Kirkcaldy
ministers

1645
Battle of
Kilsyth, over
250 Kirkcaldy
men died

Late Medieval

Stuart Britain

1437-60
James II

1460-88
James III

1488-1513
James IV

1513-42
James V

1542-67
Mary
Queen of
Scots

1567-1603
James VI   (becomes)

1603-25
James I of
England

1638
National
Covenant

1642-49
Civil War

1833
Many die of
cholera in
Kirkcaldy and
Dysart

1847
Railway
comes to
Kirkcaldy

1854
Guns made
for the
Crimean War

1879
Tay Bridge
Disaster

1892
Beveridge
Park opens

1901
Kirkcaldy
Police Station
opens

1790
Adam Smith
dies in
Edinburgh

1792
Robert
Adam dies
in London

Georgian Era

Victorian Britain

1790
Forth and
Clyde Canal
opened

1804
Invention of
the power
loom

1815
Battle of
Waterloo

1833
Burgh
Reform
Act

1840
Rise of
Chartism

1854-6
Crimean
War

1876
Telephone
invented

1887
Queen
Victoria's
Golden
Jubilee

1899-1902
Boer War

1837-1901
Queen Victoria

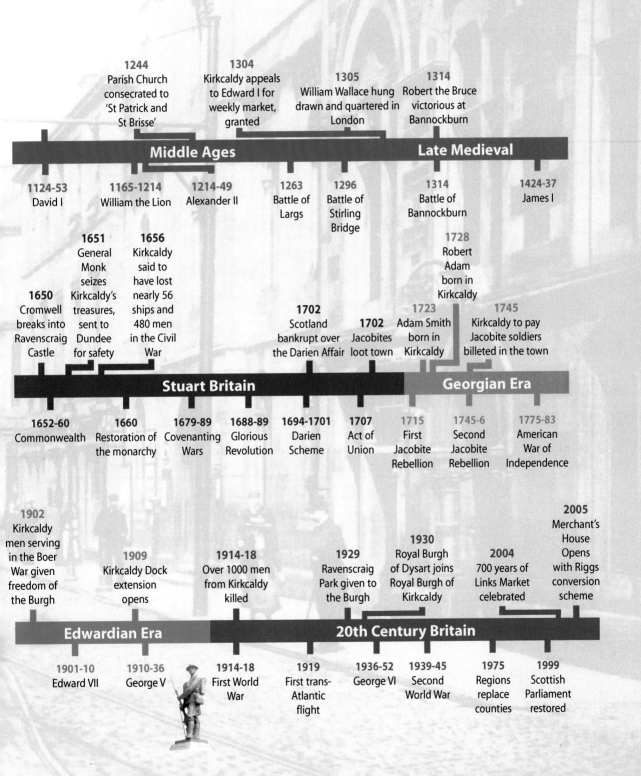

1244
Parish Church consecrated to 'St Patrick and St Brisse'

1304
Kirkcaldy appeals to Edward I for weekly market, granted

1305
William Wallace hung drawn and quartered in London

1314
Robert the Bruce victorious at Bannockburn

Middle Ages

Late Medieval

1124-53
David I

1165-1214
William the Lion

1214-49
Alexander II

1263
Battle of Largs

1296
Battle of Stirling Bridge

1314
Battle of Bannockburn

1424-37
James I

1651
General Monk seizes Kirkcaldy's treasures, sent to Dundee for safety

1656
Kirkcaldy said to have lost nearly 56 ships and 480 men in the Civil War

1728
Robert Adam born in Kirkcaldy

1650
Cromwell breaks into Ravenscraig Castle

1702
Scotland bankrupt over the Darien Affair

1702
Jacobites loot town

1723
Adam Smith born in Kirkcaldy

1745
Kirkcaldy to pay Jacobite soldiers billeted in the town

Stuart Britain

Georgian Era

1652-60
Commonwealth

1660
Restoration of the monarchy

1679-89
Covenanting Wars

1688-89
Glorious Revolution

1694-1701
Darien Scheme

1707
Act of Union

1715
First Jacobite Rebellion

1745-6
Second Jacobite Rebellion

1775-83
American War of Independence

1902
Kirkcaldy men serving in the Boer War given freedom of the Burgh

1909
Kirkcaldy Dock extension opens

1914-18
Over 1000 men from Kirkcaldy killed

1929
Ravenscraig Park given to the Burgh

1930
Royal Burgh of Dysart joins Royal Burgh of Kirkcaldy

2004
700 years of Links Market celebrated

2005
Merchant's House Opens with Riggs conversion scheme

Edwardian Era

20th Century Britain

1901-10
Edward VII

1910-36
George V

1914-18
First World War

1919
First trans-Atlantic flight

1936-52
George VI

1939-45
Second World War

1975
Regions replace counties

1999
Scottish Parliament restored

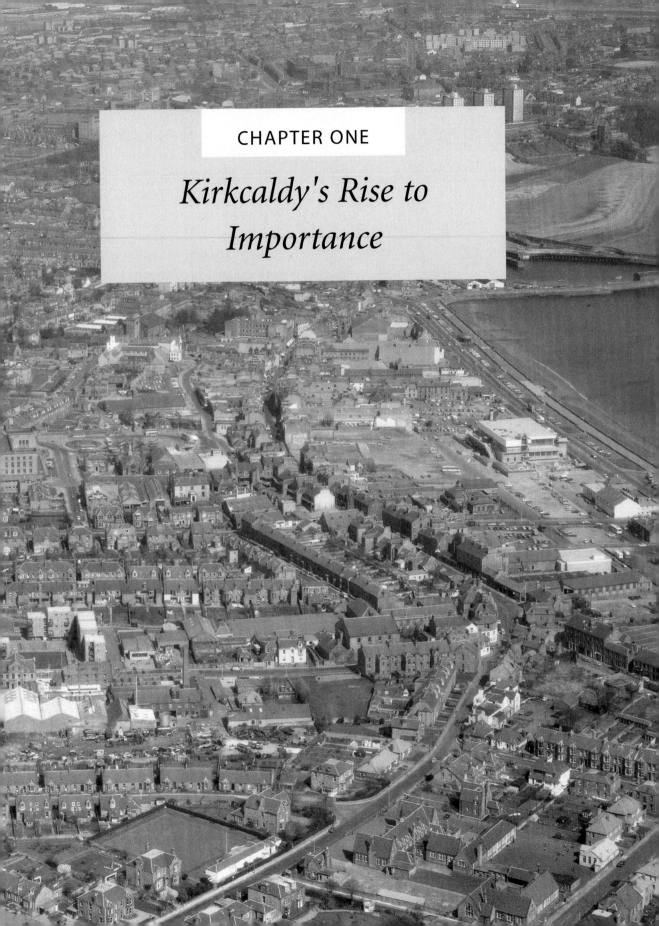

CHAPTER ONE

Kirkcaldy's Rise to Importance

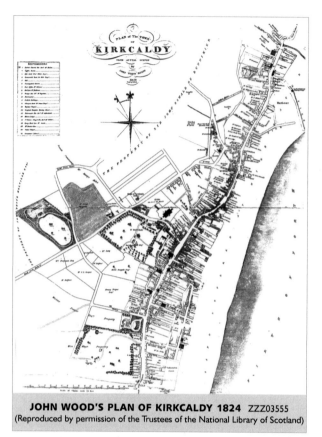

JOHN WOOD'S PLAN OF KIRKCALDY 1824 ZZZ03555
(Reproduced by permission of the Trustees of the National Library of Scotland)

Kirkcaldy includes the subsidiary villages of Linktown, Pathhead, Sinclairtown and Gallatown, which combined with the Royal Burgh in 1876 and the Royal Burgh of Dysart, which joined in 1930.

KIRKCALDY TODAY is a town of 45,000 people on the south coast of Fife, overlooking the Firth of Forth, once known as the Lang Toun because the settlement was along the coastline. There are magnificent views across the Forth to Edinburgh and the Lothians with Inchkeith Island nearby. About 1830 Thomas Carlyle described the shore as: 'The beach of Kirkcaldy in summer twilight, a mile of the smoothest sand, with one long wave coming on gently, steadily and breaking into a gradual explosion beautifully sounding and advancing ran from the south to the north, from West Burn to Kirkcaldy Harbour, a favourite scene, beautiful to me still in the far away.' He also described the people as: 'The Kirkcaldy population were a pleasant honest kind of fellow mortalism something of the quietly fruitful good old Scotch in their works and ways.' Indeed a good introduction to this town.

Kirkcaldy could mean 'Kirk of the Culdees', the early Scottish church, before Scotland became Roman Catholic from the 11th century, due to the influence of Queen Margaret (later St Margaret), wife of King Malcolm Canmore. The Culdee Church was probably on the site of the present Old Parish Church. There are a few pointers to the very earliest inhabitants of Kirkcaldy. Eleven Bronze Age cist burials have been found on five Kirkcaldy sites dated between 2500 and 5000 BC.

There is the unmarked Bogely or Dysart Standing Stone to the east of the A92 on the road north. It has recently been temporarily moved owing to opencast mining and four Bronze Age burials were found around it, dated about 4000 BC.

There is a little evidence of the Romans having been near Kirkcaldy. However, many Roman coins have been found in gardens in the town and the Romans were thought to have had camps at Carberry and Chapel to the north of Kirkcaldy.

About six miles along the coast to the northeast are the famous Wemyss Caves with their Pictish and Viking drawings. There is also an earlier drawing of cup marks said to be dated about 2000 BC. The Picts were active from AD 500 to AD 900. There is a sculptured Pictish stone at Dogtown about four miles north of Kirkcaldy. Time Team had a recent dig in and around the Wemyss Caves with a programme broadcast in February 2005.

One of the earliest records we have was of the Battle of Raith in AD 596, which some

Did you know?

The early Christians in Scotland were known as the Culdees. They were superseded in the 11th century by the Roman Catholics, who were overthrown by John Knox in the 16th century to be replaced by Presbyterianism.

A DRAWING FROM WEMYSS CAVES ZZZ03859

A perpendicular fish – an early Christian symbol – with two cup marks.

say was around Raith Hill to the west of Kirkcaldy's Mill Dam. The battle was with the Angles, who left their galleys on the shore and hastened to fight against King Aidan's supporters – the Picts, Scots and Britons. One night King Aidan's men feasted merrily and at daybreak charged into the enemy camp, where unfortunately they were swallowed up and the battle won by the Angles. King Aidan was King of Dalriada, in the west of Scotland, from AD 574. He was the first of the Celtic kings from whom the Stuart kings were directly descended.

The Vikings came to Scotland in 794 and landed in Dysart and elsewhere along the Fife coast, making their way inland, killing, burning and destroying churches. For a while there was much slaughter, but later there was some fraternisation and friendly relations were firmly established by 1000; some Vikings even married Scottish lassies as is evidenced from some of the findings in the Wemyss Caves. For example two rings were found in one of the caves, one from a Viking husband to his Scottish bride and one with a thistle from a Scottish bride to her Viking husband.

Kirkcaldy was bounded on the south by the Tiel Burn and to the north by the Den Burn. These like gates were used to control the movement of the population. The town was in a good position on the coast with what became an excellent harbour.

The Norman invasion of England took place in 1066 and William the Conqueror won the Battle of Hastings. Edgar Atheling, claimant to the throne, and his sister Margaret did not return to Hungary where they had originally come from, but their ship was 'blown off course' and they landed in Fife and proceeded to Dunfermline where shortly afterwards, in 1069, Margaret became the second wife of Malcolm Canmore, King of Scotland. She was a very Christian lady and a follower of the Roman Catholic faith. She found the Culdee Church too simple and so she introduced Roman Catholicism to Scotland, which eventually replaced the simple Culdee religion. Roman Catholicism remained the main Scottish religion for nearly 500 years until the Reformation. Queen Margaret built a church in Dunfermline, which eventually became an abbey and pilgrims came pouring into Fife, bound for St Andrews. She set up a ferry at what is now called Queensferry, to assist pilgrims to cross the Forth.

From 1075 Malcolm Canmore decreed the giving of the 'shire of Kirkcaladunt and other gifts' to Dunfermline and so Kirkcaldy was bound to pay dues and taxes to support the church there. The Dunfermline church was made an abbey by David I (1124–1153), son of Queen Margaret. The Abbot's hall in Kirkcaldy, a retreat for the Abbot of Dunfermline stood close to today's Abbotshall Church – some of the walls are still visible around the houses of Raith Estate.

In 1451 the Abbot of Dunfermline ceded to the Bailies and Council of Kirkcaldy the ports, the rents and 52 acres of Kirkcaldy land. This brought money into Kirkcaldy for development when previously a considerable amount was passing to Dunfermline for the upkeep of the Abbey. Over the years the church had become both very wealthy and

Kirkcaldy has its own castle, Ravenscraig, commissioned in 1460 by James II and built with thick stone walls to fight off invaders with returning gunfire, having gun loops instead of arrow slits. Sadly the 29-year-old James was killed by an accidental explosion of a cannon near Floors Castle in the Borders. His widowed Queen, Mary of Guelders, continued with the building of the Castle and was said to have had a great time with 'every other woman's husband'. Then she died and the castle passed to James III who was only a minor at the time. When he became king in his own right he did not want this castle, being more anxious to have the Northern Isles of Orkney and Shetland back in the Kingdom of Scotland.

The Earl of Caithness, originally from Normandy, then known as William de Santa Clara, had been granted lands at Roslin near Edinburgh from William the Conquerer. William, the 3rd Earl, received the Earldom of Caithness in 1455 and had married a Norwegian princess, who brought as a part of her dowry the Northern Isles, which had remained in Viking control. James donated the castle to the Earl and demanded the Northern Isles in exchange. Thus the Earl of Caithness, a Sinclair, owned the castle and the area around became known as Sinclairtown or St Clair. Today the Earl of Rosslyn is the superior of much of the land in this part of Kirkcaldy.

There is a story of the Lady Rosabelle from the castle who, sometime between 1530 and 1600, was invited to a party at Roslin Castle and set off despite a warning:

Ravenscraig Castle

'Moor, moor the barge ye gallant crew
And gentle lady's deign to stay
Rest thee in Castle Ravensheugh
Nor tempt the stormy Forth today.

Last night the gifted seer did see
A wet shroud swathed round Lady's gay
Then stay thee fair maid in Ravensheugh
Why cross the Forth today.'

Sir Walter Scott, 'Lay of the Last Minstrel'.

She set off for the visit but sadly drowned in the Forth. A street in Kirkcaldy known as Rosabelle Street is named after the lady of this sad story.

RAVENSCRAIG CASTLE 2000 KR00001k

The castle has been restored by Historic Scotland and the entrance is always open although the chambers are locked.

Ravenscraig Castle gave refuge to the Earl of Huntly in 1592, the escaping murderer of the Bonnie Earl of Moray. In those days it was not considered good manners to deny hospitality to a person of equal standing, whatever they had been up to.

When the Castle was no longer required for defence the Earl of Rosslyn decided to build a house nearby – The Hermitage – the castle being used then as a store and granary. Sadly, The Hermitage caught fire in 1722 but was rebuilt by 1726 and is known today as Dysart House. In 1896 Dysart House was bought by Michael Barker Nairn, later Sir Michael. The house was sold in 1929 to the Coates of Paisley who donated it to the Roman Catholic Church. It opened in 1930 as a Carmellite Monastry for nuns.

In 1929 the grounds – the Three Trees Park – were gifted to the town of Kirkcaldy, and became known as Ravenscraig Park, Kirkcaldy's second large park – the other being Beveridge Park, which opened in 1892. The Three Trees Park got its name from the story that three Sinclair brothers were walking home one pitch-dark night. They thought they were being attacked and out came their swords. When morning came they were all dead. No one had attacked them but in the dark they imagined they had been set upon and had killed each other. Three trees were planted nearby in their memory; only one still stands since recent storms.

corrupt. Henry VIII broke with the Church of Rome over his second marriage in 1533, claiming that his first marriage was illegal, as he had married his widowed sister-in-law; he then made himself the head of the Church in England. John Knox had more Christian motives for disassociating with Rome and eventually became powerful enough to overthrow the Catholic Church.

The area around Kirkcaldy contains many castles. Balwearie Tower, a ruin on the edge of the town, was the 'castle' home of the Scott family. This castle was not built until the 15th century, but may have been built on the site of an earlier wooden structure. In 1280 Michael Scott of Balwearie was granted by the Abbot of Dunfermline the Mill Pool at Kirkcaldy, and the coast between Balwearie and Invertiel and the 'milntoun'. There have been several 'Michael Scotts' and probably the legend has intertwined more than one. Michael was a learned man who had studied abroad. He had great mystical powers and became known as the 'Wizard of Balwearie'. A Michael Scott was sent to Norway to bring the eight-year-old Maid Margaret to Scotland in 1296 after Alexander III tragically died riding home one dark night, when his horse fell over the cliff near Kinghorn. Sadly the Maid died before she reached Scotland.

Seafield Tower, a tower of defence, is found on the coast, close to the large new Seafield housing estate. The Tower was built around 1520 by the Moutray family, but there were continual feuds between them and the Melvilles of Raith. One of the Moutrays was killed by one of the Melvilles, so the latter

were ordered to pay each year for a mass to be said for the dead man's soul. The Tower was inhabited until 1733 and became a ruin after this time, passing to the Fergusons of Raith.

Piteadie Castle, built in the 16th century, is now a ruin on the southern edge of the town. There is a gateway with the date 1686 and initials WC, as the building was at that time owned by William Calderhead, apothecary and burgess of Edinburgh.

Big houses were built from the late 17th century. In 1684 Alexander Lord Raith, oldest son of the First Lord Melville, built Raith House for his bride Barbara Dundas. The house still stands today in extensive grounds, though much of the estate has been sold for housing and new roads. The Melvilles sold Raith to the Ferguson family in 1707. Today Richard Munro-Ferguson inhabits the house.

In 1692 John Watson of Burntisland built Dunnikier House at the top of the Path for his bride Euphan Orrock. The area around John Watson's house was then known as Dunnikier. He soon ran out of cash and in 1703 sold the house to Captain James Oswald who probably made the bulk of his fortune from privateering, a form of piracy then acceptable in naval terms. In 1790 General Sir John Oswald built the new Dunnikier House to the north of the town, now the Dunnikier Hotel. The area around the old house then became known as Pathhead and the house as Path House, while the new Dunnikier House area became Dunnikier. The Path House has had various uses and after standing empty for a few years in a ruinous state was renovated and is now a doctors' surgery.

PATH HOUSE ZZZ03860

PATH HOUSE 2005 ZZZ03860

Built in 1692, this was originally known as Dunnkier House.

Other big houses have been built by industrialists: The Lions House, built by the Methvens of the Linktown Pottery; Adelaide House, built by George Elder, banker, whose sons emigrated to Australia (best known – Sir Thomas Elder); Gladney House, built in 1711 by William Adam, father of Robert Adam, and Viewforth Tower, built in 1790 for Robert Pratt, a local linen manufacturer, and probably designed by one of the Adam brothers. None of these have survived. However, St Brycedale House, built for George Heggie around 1786, is now known as Hunter House and has become the centrepiece of a flatted complex for older people. It was probably designed by Robert Adam and features several round rooms.

By the 18th and 19th centuries there was much trade overseas. If you were a ship owner you were interested in when your ship was coming home and so many houses were

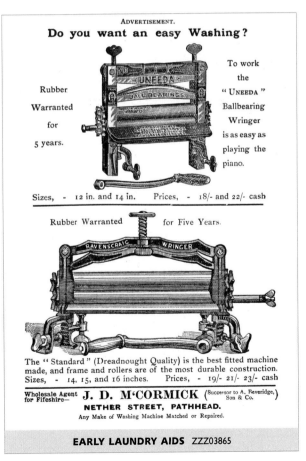

EARLY LAUNDRY AIDS ZZZ03865

built with towers. Later it seemed that the tower became a status symbol whether or not you were a shipowner or could view the sea. Viewforth Tower had a tower and was also thought to have had a tunnel to the shore to aid smugglers. Other towers may still be seen in houses around the town: Beechwood, once the home of Provost Michael Beveridge; Tower Villa (later named Stairard) in Wemyssfield; and Harbour House, opposite the Harbour.

CHURCH AND STATE

There was probably a Culdee cell on the site of the present Old Parish Church. The church was then rebuilt as a Roman Catholic Church, which remained the religion of Scotland until John Knox and the Reformation established a Presbyterian Protestant faith. However, in 1244 the parish church was consecrated by Bishop de Bernham to St Brisse and St Patrick, the latter name being later dropped. St Brisse was a follower of St Martin of Tours in France and became his successor in 397, when he became the Bishop of Tours. He never visited Kirkcaldy.

Prior to the Reformation, there was trouble in Fife involving the French Catholic army of Mary of Lorraine, Queen Regent and mother of Mary Queen of Scots. She arrived with the French fleet and took St Andrews Castle. John

THE HARBOUR c1905 KR00003

Ships with steam and sail are seen in the harbour, with many factory chimneys in the background.

Knox was captured by French troops and was forced to row a galley ship for two years before returning to Scotland. Many martyrs were burnt in St Andrews, including George Wishart in 1546 and shortly afterwards, by way of retaliation, Cardinal Beaton was murdered. A battle was fought near Cupar between the Queen Regent's army and the Lords of the Congregation, those determined for a Protestant faith. The Queen Regent's French troops set fire to Kirkcaldy in 1559.

Meantime Kirkcaldy grew as an ecclesiastical burgh under the control of the Church, and eventually became powerful enough to overthrow the Catholic Church.

After the Reformation there were no ministers to take the Presbyterian services until more had been trained. The church of St Brisse was used as a workplace, with horses stabled inside. There was also a Masonic Lodge of St Brisse and Provost Ford had to become a member before he could lay the foundation stone of the new parish church in 1808. Only the tower of the original older building has survived.

After the Reformation the Church took on many civil responsibilities and the Elders dictated to the community as can be seen from 'The Presbytrie Booke of Kirkcaldie', which has recorded minutes from 1630 to 1653. Fornication and witchcraft seemed to be the major offences. Punishment was by way of a fine and castigation in front of the congregation for sins of fornication, and for witchcraft – often death. Drunkenness, petty thieving and a breach of the Sabbath were also censored.

Witchcraft was a problem in Scotland and witches were persecuted from 1563 until 1736. The last witch was put to death in Scotland in 1727 in Sutherland. In 1633 Alison Dick and her husband William Coke were burned at the stake in Kirkcaldy, a year when many Fife witches were burned. One entry states: 'Sept. 1638 Margaret Greig was contained in the steeple on suspicion of witchcraft. Nothing could be found against her and she was dismissed'. In 1666, Grissell Wilsone was called before the session for abusing Thomas Allan and his spouse. Witnesses were called and said that Grissell had called the spouse of Thomas Allan an 'evil favoured shitten toad…'. Grissell was admonished and warned that if she ever was found to be the like again she would sustain strict and public censure.

Although Charles I had been king since 1625 he arranged a Scottish Coronation in 1633, and he created Kirkcaldy a Royal Burgh in 1644 when 8.12 acres of common land was given to the people of Kirkcaldy for the 'bleaching of linen, drying of clothes and for recreation, in perpetuity'.

There was strife within the Presbyterian

Did you know?

Charles I and Charles II were both crowned in Scotland: Charles I in Edinburgh in 1633 after he was crowned in England in 1625, and Charles II in Scone in 1651 before he was crowned in England in 1660.

Church during the reign of Charles I (1625–49), against the introduction of bishops, episcopacy and patronage (the heritors not the congregation choosing the minister). The Kirkcaldy churches rebelled against this – the time of the Covenanters had arrived. In Scotland the Solemn League and Covenant to protect Presbyterianism was signed in Greyfriars Church in Edinburgh in 1638. The Rev George Gillespie, who was born in Kirkcaldy where his father was the minister, was among those who went to London to sign the Westminster Confession in 1644. Sadly, George Gillespie died in 1648, when only 36 years of age, and was buried in Kirkcaldy. Archbishop Sharp ordered his grave to be destroyed. However, a new stone was erected inside the south porch of the parish church in 1746. Archbishop Sharp was murdered by Covenanters on Magus Muir in 1679.

In 1639 all freemen and burgesses were to be trained in drilling and the use of arms, to enable them to fight to defend the faith with General Leslie as head of the Covenanting army. In 1645 the Covenanters suffered a great defeat at the Battle of Kilsyth, when Kirkcaldy lost over 250 men. Later, as a result of the Civil War, 480 Kirkcaldy men were killed and most of the 56 ships belonging to the town were destroyed. All this affected the economy, which took many years to build up again. This was indeed a great setback for Kirkcaldy trade – no ships and few men, the population being just over 3,000. By 1656 Kirkcaldy had 12 ships left in the harbour, of which only half belonged to townsmen.

THE PAST ROYAL BURGH COAT OF ARMS
ZZZ03861

The Coat of Arms embroidered on curtains in the Town House. There was the Abbey of Dunfermline with sometimes a man at the door, St Brisse, Patron Saint of Kirkcaldy. The town motto was 'Vigilando Munio' ('I guard by watching'). The coat of arms established in 1673 represented Kirkcaldy until the town became part of Kirkcaldy District in 1975.

In 1649 Charles I was beheaded and the country became a Commonwealth, and then a Protectorate under Oliver Cromwell. There were no bishops under Cromwell's Puritan regime. Cromwell came to Kirkcaldy in 1650. He needed somewhere to lodge his troops and so broke into Ravenscraig Castle, then used as a granary, where he found food in plenty and shelter. Other solders were billeted in the town at the town's expense, each soldier being paid 4d a day by the town (less than 2p). Cromwell was known to have lodged his horses in the parish church. Explosives had been stored in Dysart's 1576 Tolbooth, which was consequently badly damaged by an accidental explosion in 1656. Kirkcaldy's

THE DYSART TOLBOOTH 2005 KI9770Ik

This was built in 1576 and was once the centre of the Royal Burgh of Dysart, with cells to lock up wrongdoers.

navy in the war against the Dutch. The men were to be volunteers or if necessary, 'pressed'. In 1665 victory was recorded over the Dutch fleet, and in 1667 a second victory.

All the people of Kirkcaldy were expected to attend church on the Sabbath, but there are many instances of salters working on the saltpans and being dealt with later, salting being an important local industry. In 1645 all persons leaving before the blessing were to be fined six shillings; at that time sermons could be very long and six shillings was a lot of money.

The unpopular system of patronage was abolished in 1690 but was reintroduced by Queen Anne in 1722. This led to the Secession of the Church in 1733 and the new secession church established in Kirkcaldy in 1737 was known as Bethelfield. A second church exodus, for much the same reason as the first, known as the Disruption, occurred in 1843 and resulted in the parish church losing two-thirds of the congregation. A new free church was built in Tolbooth Street in 1844, but in 1881 the congregation moved to their new building St Brycedale, and St Brisse Parish Church became the Old Parish Church. Now, the two congregations have merged and the complex is known as St Bryce Kirk with the old church being the place of worship and the other for meetings with a popular café. As both are known as St Bryce, one often wonders which one to enter!

town treasures had been sent to Dundee for safety but these were found and taken by General Monk in 1651.

Cromwell died in 1660, the monarchy was restored and Charles II returned from exile in France. He had been crowned King in Scotland in 1651 and had promised to respect Presbyterianism. However, he had not been long on the throne officially when he reneged and again forced the issue of patronage, bishops and archbishops on the Scots. In 1664, the Town Council was responsible for organising 20 sailors to serve in the King's

Did you know?

After the Jacobite Uprising of 1745 Catholics were banned and Episcopalians were allowed to worship in groups of no more than six. They would meet in a house and there would be six in several rooms – the rector in the hall or moving around. The regulations were relaxed before the end of the 18th century and a small church was built in 1813. Numbers grew and a larger building was needed which opened in 1844.

ST PETER'S EPISCOPAL CHURCH 1844–1975
KR00004

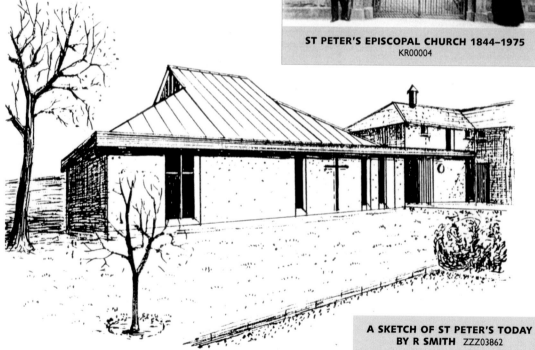

**A SKETCH OF ST PETER'S TODAY
BY R SMITH** ZZZ03862

The old church had to be demolished because of subsidence due to uncharted underground mining, and a new one was built close by which was dedicated in 1976.

EDUCATION

The early reformed Church was concerned about education, and appointed the schoolmaster and inspected the schools. From early times there were some church/parish schools and John Knox's dream was for every parish to have its own school so that there would be universal education long before this was so in England.

The Burgh School was established in the 16th century, but a new school was built in Hill Street in 1725. Adam Smith and Robert Adam were pupils at that school and from 1816 until 1818 Thomas Carlyle was the schoolmaster (see Chapter Three). However, Carlyle did not enjoy teaching, but made friends with Edward Irving (then master at a rival subscription school in Oswald Wynd) who became a great charismatic preacher. Edward Irving returned to Kirkcaldy to preach the evening sermon in 1828. The new church building had been finished in rather a hurry and it is thought that some of the gallery timbers had not had time to season. As Edward Irving entered the church the crowd in the gallery rushed forward to look at him and sadly the gallery collapsed, killing 28 people and injuring 150. The Burgh School remained in Hill Street until a new grammar school was built in St Brycedale Avenue in 1843.

Prior to the Education Act Scotland 1872, Kirkcaldy had subscription schools, female schools, industrial and adventure schools (apprentice schools), Philp schools from 1830

LINKTOWN PHILP SCHOOL c1960 KR00005

(see Did you know? box below) and half time schools for children working in industry. All this changed when the school boards were established after 1872 with compulsory school attendance for children aged 5–13. Education became the responsibility of the local council, with only a few private schools remaining – mostly dame schools. In 1894 Sir Michael Barker Nairn extended the Grammar School and had a bust of himself put up over the entrance to the Assembly Hall so that pupils would be aware of his generosity!

THE CASTLE O'GUNS STONE ZZZ03863

'Gif thankis unto The Lord 1585'. The stone was in thanks for the ending of the plague in Dysart. It was taken from the tall 1584 building on Howard Place, demolished in 1955, and placed into the new municipal houses built there.

Did you know?

Three Philp schools were built in Kirkcaldy with money from the Robert Philp Trust. Most had closed by 1890. The Linktown school opened in 1830 and closed in 1891. Pupils at these schools were known as Philpers. This building had various uses after 1891, but was eventually demolished in 1964.

HEALTH

In 1584 the plague struck the town, brought in by a Dutch ship. The Council laid down certain rules: people with the plague were to be isolated in their homes and if any attempt was made by anyone to escape from the town, they were first to be branded and later to be put to death, if again caught. Later plague victims were taken to the Burgh Muir for isolation. A guard was put on all bridges to prevent people leaving the town. Over 300 died of the plague in Kirkcaldy and many in Dysart. Kirkcaldy did not have another severe outbreak, even when the plague was raging in London in 1665.

In 1832 cholera broke out in Kirkcaldy due to the water being polluted with sewage. Many people died and were hastily buried. Provost William Swan was one who died in 1833 and his son, Provost Patrick Don Swan, instigated a clean water supply for the people of Kirkcaldy in 1867.

Michael Barker Nairn gifted the Cottage Hospital in 1890 and extended it a few years later. The new Fever Hospital was opened in 1899 and is today a part of the Victoria Hospital. In 1808 prayers were said here for Dr Jenner, inventor of smallpox vaccinations.

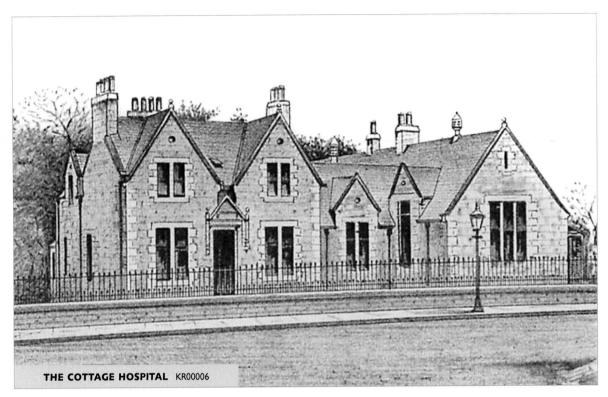

THE COTTAGE HOSPITAL KR00006

The Cottage Hospital opened in 1890, and was donated by Sir Michael Barker Nairn, son of Michael Nairn.

Did you know?

Both James V and James VI of Scotland sent ships from Kirkcaldy to collect their brides. In 1536 James V sailed from Kirkcaldy to collect his first wife Madeleine from France and in 1589 James VI sent the ship 'Angel' from Kirkcaldy to bring back his betrothed, Anne of Denmark.

HARBOUR

The Council was responsible for the harbour and for raising money to have it repaired, since it was frequently damaged by storms. At one time a levy of 2d (less than 1p) a pint was put on beer to raise money for harbour repairs. Many wives made beer to escape the tax, but this was illegal as all beer had to be made by the official brewers. In 1664 the Provost was fined for brewing his own beer!

In 1591 the sailors established the Prime Gilt Box. Money was put in the box and given to families when a sailor had died or was suffering extreme hardship. There were three locks and three keys held by three different men. That box is today in Kirkcaldy Museum and there is a street known as Prime Gilt Box Street.

In 1733 there were ferries sailing to Leith, while the first steamboat ferries started in 1820. The harbour was extended in 1909 to cope with steamships as West Wemyss and Dysart harbours were too small. In 1808 the Kirkcaldy, Leith and Glasgow Steam Packet Company, the Pinnace, opened and the little boats made their way to the west via the Forth and Clyde Canals.

The railway came to Kirkcaldy in 1847 with additional stations in Dysart and Sinclairtown. However, the ferry from Burntisland completed the journey to Edinburgh until the Forth Rail Bridge opened in 1890, giving a direct route to Edinburgh. Kirkcaldy boomed.

NATIONAL AND LOCAL AFFAIRS

In 1603, as a result of the Union of the Crowns after the death of Elizabeth Tudor, James VI of Scotland became James I of Britain. He only returned once to Scotland in 1617. In 1707 there was the Union of the Parliaments. Scotland was at this time in debt owing to the Darian Affair, 1698–1700, a disastrous investment into land around where the Panama Canal is today, with shares sold nationwide. It was thought it would bring in much money; instead, it was a disaster as men died of yellow fever and the Spanish and English were against the Scots establishing a settlement. Negotiations went ahead with England, and the Scots agreed to give up their parliament; in exchange religion and laws were to remain essentially Scottish. The Union led to many changes, with local taxes being sent to England, which many

resented, leading to much smuggling, which continued for over 150 years.

Kirkcaldy was expanding at this time, so Linktown of Abbotshall was made into a

separate parish in 1651, and the first parish church in Abbotshall was built in 1674. Kirkcaldy had no Provost until 1658 as the Council thought that the bailies, councillors and magistrates could organise affairs without one. However, in 1658 the first Provost was elected, Robert Whyt, or Quyte. The tolbooth, or town hall with a prison, had been rebuilt

HIGH STREET AND THE OLD TOLBOOTH
c1920 KR00002

in Tolbooth Street in 1678 and remained there until the new Town House was opened on the High Street in 1832 where Marks & Spencer is today.

Before the smaller Burghs of Barony, Linktown of Abbotshall, Pathhead, Gallatown and Sinclairtown joined with Kirkcaldy in 1876 there were trade restrictions, and people not belonging to the Royal Burgh were not allowed to come in to sell their wares at the fairs or markets. Much trade had been done in the past at the Mercat Cross, which had been close to where Kirk Wynd joins the High Street. This was removed in 1782 when:

'*Kirkcaldy pair people*
Took doon the Cross
Tae build the steeple'

In 1304 permission had been given for the first annual fair in Links Street. From this the Links Market evolved, culminating in the celebration of 700 years of the market in 2004. The market started as a seller's market and a social meeting point. Now the Links Market is all pleasure. It comes to the town every April and there is one mile of pleasure ground, the longest street fair in Britain.

Volunteers' Green was part of over 8 acres of Common Muir given to the people of Kirkcaldy in 1644 when Charles I made Kirkcaldy a Royal Burgh. Successive Provosts and Town Councils sold off the land. In 1754 two-thirds was sold or feued to Provost Robert Whyte. The Green was first known as Volunteers' Green when the volunteer movement was officially started in 1859 and the men drilled there. There was no Esplanade in those days; the sea washed up across the Sands Road. Four cannon were placed in front of the Green and remained there until 1901 when the Volunteers moved to Kinghorn. Two of the cannon were donated to the Beveridge Park, but vanished during the Second World War, when all metals were acquired by the government, later found to be useless and after the war dumped into the North Sea.

The Council resolved to retain one-third of the Green, then to keep one-sixth 'green'. However, the town was expanding into Nicol Street or Newtown and new stables and a police station were required. The Council

THE GEORGE HOTEL 1875 ACCOUNT ZZZ03858

This hotel was on the High Street. Stagecoaches would halt here and change horses.

VOLUNTEERS DRILLING IN FRONT OF VOLUNTEERS' GREEN WITH CANNON 1861 ZZZ03864

acquired more land and built on it. In 1879 James Graham brought an action against the Council for this new acquisition, demanding the retention of the land where there were new buildings, and won. However, the Council was reluctant to demolish their new buildings and in the end settlement was made for an extra piece of ground in Nicol Street, a short distance from Volunteers' Green, the total now covering only half an acre. Today the extra ground has been named Fraser's Green by Kirkcaldy Civic Society, which put up a plaque in memory of Mrs Minnie Fraser, late Honorary President of the Society, without whom Volunteers' Green would never have been saved from development. After many years the Green has been landscaped with a plaque in the centre, which tells the story of this most important part of Kirkcaldy's history. It is now a quiet oasis in the middle of the busy town centre.

Kirkcaldy's story continues into the era of the 20th century with sections on important people and the industrial developments before the last chapter looks forward to the future of the town.

VOLUNTEERS' GREEN FROM THE MULTI-STOREY CAR PARK 2005 K197702k (James Christie)

THE MAN I' THE ROCK 1851 KR00007

A Dysart weaver, John Paterson, carved The Man in the Rock in 1851. It represented Byron's Prisoner of Chillon. Sadly, these rocks, just north of the town, were washed away by the sea in 1971.

CHAPTER TWO

Boom Town – 1900-2000

KIRKCALDY WAS by 1900 a thriving industrial town. The linoleum industry (see Chapter four) was at its peak and the town was also renowned for its engineering and furniture manufacture.

WARS

In 1899 the Boer War started and nearly a hundred men from Kirkcaldy volunteered for action – an opportunity to see pastures new. Some lost their lives and others were injured. All who served in the forces received the Freedom of the Burgh. Peace came in 1902.

In 1914 the First World War broke out, caused by a minor event, but one that ignited and involved most of Europe. Thousands upon thousands died including over 1,000 men from Kirkcaldy, recorded on the 36 copper–bronze plates on the War Memorial unveiled in 1923.

> ## Did you know?
>
> *The North Sea was originally known as the German Ocean but after the First World War became known as the North Sea, just as the Royal family adopted the surname Windsor in 1917.*

John Nairn lost his only son Ian in the war and in his memory gifted the Museum and Art Gallery, which opened in 1925 and is now one of the best in Scotland. The building was erected on the site of Balsusney House, which

the Council had purchased for a museum before the war. Two years later, in 1927, Mr Nairn added the Library, which included the Beveridge Library, originally located in the Adam Smith Halls that opened in 1899.

The Museum and Art Gallery situated

THE MUSEUM AND ART GALLERY 1926 KR00008

The Museum and Art Gallery was opened in 1925. Behind can be seen the buildings of Barry Ostlere and Shepherd, linoleum manufacturers.

beside the main line railway station contains a collection of many famous paintings by artists Peploe and McTaggart as well as many others, which includes our local Fife Jack Vettriano. Kirkcaldy Burgh acquired other paintings in 1964 from John Blyth's private collection after he died. The linen manufacturing firm of Andrew Blyth who built Hawklymuir factory in 1854 had closed in 1960. Over a hundred paintings from the Blyth collection were purchased for a small price.

In 1939 the Second World War broke out because the Germany Britain had defeated during the First World War had been allowed to rear its head and become imperialistic – annexing nearby countries – with an additional policy of ridding Europe of all Jews and others, considered undesirable. This war was indeed fought for ideals. Over 450 who died are listed on the additional 11 copper–bronze plates of the War Memorial. Parts of Scotland were bombed during the last war, but bombs were not dropped on Kirkcaldy, although one dropped on a nearby farm killing some cattle, and a few fell in other parts of Fife when returning enemy planes jettisoned unwanted cargo.

HEALTH

The century also saw many changes in health. At the close of the First World War there was a widespread influenza epidemic over the whole country and many people in Kirkcaldy died. The Cottage Hospital donated by Sir Michael Barker Nairn opened in 1890. Above the entrance were the words 'I was sick and ye visited me 1889'. The hospital was enlarged in 1897 and 1915, two round wards being added. The hospital closed in 1970, was demolished in 1985 and flats named The Kyles were built on the site, so-called after the local game bawbee-she-kyles, which was played nearby.

The new Fever Hospital was opened in

Opened in 1899, the hospital consisted of several small single-storey wards with the Sanatorium added in 1910.

THE FEVER HOSPITAL 1912 KR00009

1899. In 1910 a sanatorium was built in the grounds for TB patients, a disease that was rife until new drugs saw the near demise of the disease soon after the end of the Second World War. The new Victoria Hospital was built on this site (and was found to be riddled with mine workings), the surgical block opening in 1961 and the tower block in 1967.

In 1916 John Hunter died and left his home, St Brycedale House, to be a hospital for 'poor people, not being paupers…and such poor people as are ill of an incurable disease'. It was 1936 before there was enough money generated to pay for the conversion of the building, which opened as the Hunter Hospital. The hospital continued until 1991 when it closed (see Chapter Five for present use). In 1923 the tradition of the Kirkcaldy Pageant was started to raise funds for the local hospitals. Local firms decorated floats, there were various local bands and people in fancy dress on foot collected money. In 1948, when the National Health Service was introduced, money was no longer needed for the hospitals but was given to local charities. The Langtoun Lad and Lass, who rode through Kirkcaldy in a carriage, were introduced in 1968. The pageant ceased in 1977 but was reintroduced in 2001 with the proceeds going to various charities. In 1935 Mrs Honeyman, daughter of John Nairn, gifted her home Forth Park to be a maternity home. Today the enlarged hospital includes some wards for geriatric patients. The house itself is at present closed as it is said to be unsafe.

Today the whole outlook on health has changed. As people live longer, often beyond the time they can care for themselves, so residential and nursing homes are needed for the elderly, some being converted from big houses, like Marchmont, Abbeyfield (previously known as Bennochy Park) and Station Court (formerly the Station Hotel), while others have been purpose-built.

Council Housing

After both World Wars there was a need for new housing. The first council houses were built in 1922 with many more after the Second World War, so that Kirkcaldy ceased to be the Lang Toun but spread inland, with schools, shops and churches following. Three blocks of eight-storey flats were built on the Esplanade in 1958, requiring the demolition of Viewforth Tower. In Pathhead the first of the three 15-storey blocks was opened in 1966, Pathhead West Church being demolished to make space available. The views from these fine flats are spectacular.

A VIEW OF EIGHT-STOREY FLATS FROM THE SHORE AND NORTHWEST c1970 ZZZ03856

HOUSING

Mrs Thatcher's governments saw the end of Local Authority house building with the sale of good stock local authority houses at knock-down prices. Today housing associations are building flats and houses and there are many private schemes such as the 800 planned at Chapel and a similar number now on the site of the old Seafield Colliery. Many flats are also being built, providing good profit for builders and secure living for owners, while some old buildings like churches and factories are being converted into new homes.

EDUCATION

Education has seen considerable changes over the century. The introduction of the Education Act Scotland in 1872 led to compulsory education for ages 5–13; later the leaving age was increased to 14 and in 1973 to 16, requiring more and better schools for smaller classes.

In 1952 a new junior secondary school – Templehall – was built in Kirkcaldy amongst the new local authority houses. It existed until 1972 when it became the Junior building for Kirkcaldy High School under comprehensive education. Templehall buildings were demolished in 1995 and new houses have been built on the site. The High School moved from the centre of town in 1958 to a site once part of the ground of the Oswalds of Dunnikier House. Balwearie Secondary opened in 1964, becoming a comprehensive

TEMPLEHALL JUNIOR SECONDARY SCHOOL c1954 ZZZ03866

This school opened in 1952 for pupils not going to the High School.

The school was opened in 1843, replacing the old Burgh School in Hill Street.

KIRKCALDY GRAMMAR SCHOOL 1850 KR00010

school in 1971, and very successfully covering the full range of secondary pupils. Viewforth High School built at the beginning of the 20th century was once a junior high school. There is also a Roman Catholic Primary and a High School under Local Authority control.

The move by Kirkcaldy High School from the centre of town left the adjacent listed Technical College, built in 1926, room to expand. The old school was demolished in 1964 and a nine-storey tower block opened in 1968, which was demolished in 2003 to make way for Fife College to rebuild. The College is shortly to combine with Glenrothes College, to be known as Adam Smith College. Since 1970 the College has greatly expanded in numbers and course options and now includes some degree courses in association with the University of Abertay.

HARBOUR

Kirkcaldy Harbour was a busy place for many years until 1992 when the last large ship sailed out to sea. It was said that the lock gates needed repairing and so since that time the gates have been left open and the harbour tidal used only by the local boat club. The London and Kirkcaldy Shipping Company had steamers sailing to London twice a week until 1964.

Ships came to the harbour with grain for the nearby flour mill and maltings and left with coal and linoleum. Latterly large amounts of scrap metal were exported. It is hoped that the harbour with its many new blocks of flats will soon be open to the public, many of whom in the past fished from the end of the pier, although it was rare to catch anything worth eating.

CHURCHES

Over the century there have been many changes in churches and congregations; both have aged and numbers have fallen dramatically in all but some evangelistic groups. Many churches have amalgamated, often with much angst; others are sharing ministers.

Dunnikier Union Church closed in 1928 because the building was uncomfortable. Invertiel Parish closed in 1952 joining with Invertiel Free, now combined with Bethelfield and known as Linktown while their former 'free' building is occupied by the Coptic Christians. In 1958, Pathhead West joined Pathhead East to form Pathhead Parish Church. In 1969 Loughborough Road, once a United Presbyterian, closed and was demolished except for the hall used by the Brethren. St James's Church at the Port Brae was closed in 1969 due to the building being unsafe, and was later demolished, but the minister continued to preach nearby. In 1972, Dysart Barony Church joined St Serf's Free Church to become Dysart Parish Kirk. Again in 1972, Dunnikier Church (now Roman Catholic) joined with Victoria Road to be known as St Andrews. In 1977, Gallatown, once a Free Church, joined Sinclairtown to be known as Viewforth Church. In the 1960s, St Michael's Episcopal closed and in 1979 St Columba's Episcopal became a Roman

NEW CRAIGS EVANGELICAL CHURCH 2005 KI97705k

The church opened in 1990 in an area of new houses in the north of the town.

Catholic church before later becoming a house.

A few new churches were built in new housing areas: Templehall in 1956, Torbain in 1969 and Newcraigs Evangelical in 1990. St Peter's Episcopal was rebuilt because of subsidence in 1976, and St John's, also after a fire, in 1975. Two postwar church buildings opened in Hayfield Road, now used by Churches of Christ and Hebron Gospel. The Closed Brethren built their Hall in Ferrard Road in the 1970s and bought the old Dutch Mill Restaurant, demolishing it to build a private car park. There is also a Jehovah's Witness hall, and a small hut used as a mosque.

Only non-denominational churches have remained open with shrinking congregations – Methodists, Baptists and Congregationalists.

TRANSPORT

Transport has changed dramatically over the century. In 1903 tramcars were introduced in Kirkcaldy. The new Victoria Viaduct was opened in 1902 to allow tramcars an easy journey down the town apart from the steep Path. A power station for the trams was built close to the Viaduct. Drivers were controlled by stamping time cards at clocks known as Bundy Clocks, named after the manufacturer. Kirkcaldy was now linked to the villages of Pathhead, Gallatown, Sinclairtown, Linktown and later, Dysart. Trams continued until 1931 when competition from buses drove them into the dust.

In 1900 there were few if any private cars; now the streets are lined with them at night

> ## Did you know?
>
> *The drivers of the Kirkcaldy tramcars had to punch cards along the route at Bundy Clocks to check whether they were running on time or not. There is one such Bundy Clock left on St Clair Street. Bundy was the name of the manufacturer.*

as public transport has become expensive and sometimes unreliable. The 'clippies' have disappeared and now a bus driver has to take the money and deal with problem passengers as well as drive the bus.

There were Alexander's red town buses, with an office on the Esplanade in front of Volunteers' Green, and a country bus station sited on the Esplanade from 1930 with blue Alexander buses. In 1951 shelters were built on the Esplanade but these were often abandoned when tides were running high, sometimes breaking the glass in the

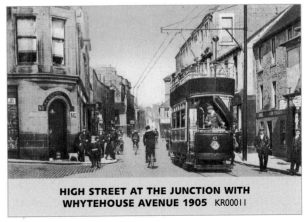

HIGH STREET AT THE JUNCTION WITH WHYTEHOUSE AVENUE 1905 KR00011

No cars can be seen – only a tram and many bicycles. The building on the left is now single-storey.

windows of the shelters. Proposals were put forward for a new town bus station in 1955 behind the Town House, but it was a few years before this materialised and it has since been redesigned for all buses, both town and

Did you know?

A day return ticket to Edinburgh in 1965 cost 7 shillings and 4d (37p). Today it costs £5.18.

country, and is due to be upgraded shortly.

The railway came to Kirkcaldy in 1847 with stations also at Dysart and Sinclairtown, which were sadly closed by the Beeching cuts in 1969. The Fife Circular Service started in 1989 with trains direct to Edinburgh, either north via Thornton or south via Kinghorn. Kirkcaldy's 1847 station was rebuilt in 1964; the southbound buildings were destroyed by fire in 1989 but reopened in 1991 with an ultra modern building. Kirkcaldy is on the main line with trains directly to London and Plymouth in the south and Aberdeen and Inverness to the north.

In 1922–23 the Sea Wall was built by unemployed men in the town and so far it has stood the test of time, being battered by the sea for over 80 years. The plaque on the wall states: '1922–1923 this Sea Wall and Esplanade were constructed by the Corporation of Kirkcaldy during the period of the great trade depression'. The money came from the Unemployment Grants Commission. This changed Sands Road where the sea used to

THE ESPLANADE STEPS IN SUMMER
1955 KR00012

This feature of the new Promenade was completed in 1923. It was a popular place in summer for swimming and sunbathing.

PROBLEMS WITH ESPLANADE FLOODING 1964 KR00013

Before the second sea wall was built in the 1980s there was often serious flooding on the Esplanade. This man was caught almost out of his depth by the rising tide after having a nap in his car following his lunch!

wash up towards the road. The Esplanade is now a busy dual carriageway. However, this means that high spring tides do come over the sea wall, sometimes causing extensive flooding, but there are intervals of several years between floods, partly due to the second inner sea wall, built at the end of 1964.

Buses and trains made travel to work easier, but then came the age of the motor car, which necessitated new roads being built, many with dual carriageways. Many people now travel long distances to and from work each day. The Forth Road Bridge opened in 1964 and the Tay Road Bridge in 1970, so Fife ceased to be an isolated peninsula. Now the roads to both bridges leading to Edinburgh and Dundee, respectively, are very busy at

peak times. The completion of the dual A92 in 1990 changed traffic patterns around the town.

Good roads mean travellers who used to stay in hotels overnight now go home. Hotel business has dropped off as many commercial travellers do not now stay away from home and many hotels have closed. The Station Hotel, which opened in 1901, closed in 1984 and opened as a Nursing Home in 1991. Anthony's Hotel closed in 1994, was demolished and a nursing home (Gowrie Bank) built on the site. The Dunnikier Arms Hotel (also known as the High Level) has become Smithy's Tavern with flats above. Many of the dinner dances once held in these hotels have now gone out of fashion in favour of discos.

DUNNIKIER HOUSE HOTEL 2005 K197706k

This house was built in 1790 for the Oswald family.

THE GREEN COCKATOO KR00014

The Green Cockatoo was the sign above a restaurant in the High Street of the same name. This was a popular eating-place from 1953 to 1987. After the building was sold the sign was removed and taken to Ayrshire.

SHOPPING

Shopping has changed over the years and there are fewer local and corner shops. Once there was the age of the travelling vans, which came round the houses, but now only the fish van survives. The last of the horse-drawn carts was replaced by a motorised van in 1988. Supermarkets have replaced many friendly local shops, but are often sited in out-of-town shopping areas. Kirkcaldy's first purpose-built supermarkets were opened in 1973/74 – Safeway at the West End and Tesco in the Mercat.

The Mercat covered shopping mall on the High Street opened in 1972, the Postings in 1979. Later in 1988, Asda opened about two and a half miles from the town centre and in 1997 the Central Retail Park opened on Chapel Farm, three miles from the town centre, with bus shelters but sadly no bus access, since there was nowhere for buses to turn!

NEWEST STYLES - - 1911

We are showing an enormous Variety of the Smartest and Most Up-to-Date Styles in Juvenile Suits at Popular Prices.

It will Repay you to Examine our Stock.

John Johnstone Limited,
The Popular Clothiers,
242 High Street,
Kirkcaldy.

BOYS SUITS 1911 ZZZ03867

A little different from today's styles!

There is two-way traffic here with the Gaumont (later known as the Odeon picture house) seen on the left. The upper parts of these buildings are little changed.

HIGH STREET c1950 KR00015

In 1965 the High Street became one-way traffic from south to north. It was pedestrianised from Whytescauseway to Kirk Wynd with fancy paving slabs and trees and was officially opened by the Convenor of Fife Regional Council, Robert Gough CBE, JP in 1991. In 1995, just before the demise of Kirkcaldy District Council, four copper bronze sculptures designed by Doug Crocker and featuring aspects of Kirkcaldy's past were sited around the High Street: one is a circular disc on a brick base with sayings of eight famous Kirkcaldy folk; another is a dome depicting eight industries once important to Kirkcaldy; another is a ring depicting 16 dates of Kirkcaldy's important events; and lastly, at the end of the pedestrianised area, a pillar with 24 addresses important to the town.

THE RING OF IMPORTANT DATES 2005 KR00016

HOLIDAYS AND LEISURE

Kirkcaldy was never a holiday town, although there was often much activity around the shore on warm summer days especially at Invertiel where there was a café, which closed around the 1920s. Pathhead Sands had a swimming float in the water and many people bathed at the Port Brae steps. Now it is rare indeed to see anyone swimming in the sea, which many suspect to be polluted, despite the new sewage works.

More leisure time means a need for more things to do. The old time dance halls like the Tudor Ballroom and the Plaza have closed. Nightclubs began to emerge. Bentleys in Nairn's old canteen, which closed in 1983, was popular for several years before closing, shortly after which the building caught fire. Several blocks of flats have been built on the site, the first being occupied in 1998. The Burma ballroom became Jackie O's, now Harlem and the old Philp School in Charlotte Street became Oscars, then Caesars, and now AD (After Dark).

The YMCA first opened in Kirkcaldy in 1886 and in 1895 moved to the Swan Memorial building at the foot of Kirk Wynd, donated by Sir Michael Nairn as a memorial to Provost Patrick Don Swan. The YM moved in 1965 to new premises in the new housing area at Valley Gardens. The YWCA started in 1915 and opened their premises on the Esplanade in 1931, with many members buying individual bricks. The building has recently been sold and the YW will be moving to rented premises meanwhile.

PATHHEAD SANDS c1950 KR00017

This was once a popular place in the summer for swimming, with a raft in the middle of the bay.

THE YWCA 2005 K197704k

The Boys Brigade thrived from 1888 in Kirkcaldy. In 1903, when the first Victoria Road Church moved to their new building, the small old building became vacant. Major Stocks who built a band hall behind, bought this. Sadly Major Stocks was killed during the First World War. The hall was sold in 2003 and has been converted into three homes. The Boys Brigade continues to meet in rented premises.

There was a greyhound racing track in Oriel Road established early in the 20th century, which closed around 1973 and was replaced by houses in Oriel Crescent.

The 20th century also saw the rise and fall of the cinema. In 1904 the first purpose-built theatre/cinema opened. It was first known as the Kings, then the Hippodrome, Opera House, Regal, ABC, Cannon, MGM and finally ABC. It closed in 2000 a few years short of its centenary, due to the multicomplex cinema that opened in Halbeath, near Dunfermline.

Pictures were at first silent movies, often with organ or piano music. From 1929 there were sound movies and later films in colour. The Palace opened in 1908, the Port Brae in 1913 and the Odeon in 1925. Other halls became converted into picture houses and just before the Second World War three more purpose-built cinemas opened over the period 1937–38, the Rio, the Raith and the Carlton. By the 1970s, when nearly every home had a television set, the cinemas began to lose custom and many of the buildings sadly burnt down – the Palace in 1945, the Carlton after becoming a bingo hall in 1972,

the Odeon on the High Street in 1975 and the Rio Bingo Hall in 1979. The latter however was quickly rebuilt and reopened. Today there is no cinema in Kirkcaldy, although the Adam Smith Theatre regularly shows good quality films.

THE PALACE CINEMA c1920 KR00018

SPORT

Despite the need to have healthy exercise it appears gyms and tanning studios seem to be most popular today. In 1936 an outdoor seawater pool, the Lido, opened at Invertiel on the site of the old chemical works. This was closed during the war years, but opened briefly afterwards, finally closing in 1953. There was a swimming club at the Harbour Basin before Provost Nicholson opened the Kirkcaldy Pool on the Esplanade in 1971. There was always a Christmas or Boxing

The cinema was a popular place until it burned down in 1945.

Day swim in the Harbour Basin for hearty folk and indeed before the new heated pool opened many people swam in the sea daily all the year round.

Cricket was at one time popular and the Kirkcaldy Club established in 1856 moved out of Beveridge Park to Bennochy Road opposite the big houses in 1957. The club remained there until 1992 when they again moved briefly to the Beveridge Park, before closing. The only cricket now played in Kirkcaldy is the Dunnikier Club, which started in 1856 in the grounds of Dunnikier House with the master, butler and coachman being keen players, and the elegant ladies interested spectators.

The Rugby Club had shared premises with the Cricket Club and the town's first football club, Kirkcaldy Wanderers, in Newton Park. When the ground was sold in 1892 to build houses in Ava Street and Novar Crescent, the rugby and cricket clubs moved into the newly constructed Beveridge Park, part of which had been the first home of Raith Rovers. The clubs then shared a brick-built pavilion until the Cricket Club moved out in 1957. Part of Newton Park with nearby Robbie's Park had been absorbed into the new Beveridge Park. The Rugby Club built a covered stand in the Beveridge Park in 1991 and in the year 2000 were promoted to the First Division. There are now five pitches and a first-class ladies team, established in 1992.

There are six tennis courts in the Beveridge Park, with a pavilion built in 1926 and five in Ravenscraig Park. However few people play on these and no schools play tennis. There is a successful private club, Kirkcaldy Lawn Tennis Club, on Boglily Road.

Raith Rovers Football Club has had a long history, starting in 1883 and becoming a senior club in 1889. On their eviction from Robbie's Park they became tenants of the ten-year old playing field owned by Robert Stark, town councillor and licensed victualler. Stark's Park was part of a local grazing area and when the crowd invaded the playing pitch during a match in 1887, a bull was released from its pen at the north end of the field and soon cleared the pitch!

The club joined the professional ranks in 1892 and had a chequered career including a shipwreck off the Canary Islands when on a close-season tour in 1922. The Depression years of the 1920s and 1930s saw a grim struggle for survival, but in 1937/38 they set a British goalscoring record of 142 goals in 34 League games.

The 1950s were a golden era for the club and a record attendance of 31,306 packed into Stark's Park for a cup-tie with Hearts in February 1953. They were relegated in 1963 and the next 30 years saw only a brief spell in the top division before they reached the Premier Division in 1993. In 1994 they won the Scottish League Cup (Coca Cola Cup) and there was indeed 'dancing in the streets of Raith' (no such place) — a celebrated misinformed comment by a football commentator. The Cup success and six matches in European competition the following season hastened the reconstruction of the ground into an all-seater stadium, but the club has once again struggled over the last decade.

COCA COLA CUP PROGRAMME 1994 ZZZ03868

to have its own club at Balwearie on ground from Raith Estate. In 1963, a municipal course opened on the grounds of Dunnikier House, which had been purchased by Kirkcaldy Burgh in 1945. It was in part to make up for the closure of the Dysart Club.

Bowling has been popular since the mid 19th century and there are many private and municipal clubs in the town with one in each of the big parks. Kirkcaldy Bowling Club was established in 1856 on ground purchased from Osborne House, home of Stocks, linen manufacturer. There is now much encouragement for young people to take up this sport.

Golf is also popular. Dysart Golf Club opened in 1898, but was partly closed during the war for the cultivation of vegetables. The Club finally closed in 1963 and the land was sold to the Council for new housing and an extension to Dysart Cemetery. In 1904 Kirkcaldy was able

THE PEOPLES' INSTITUTE ZZZ03869

Snooker and billiards are increasingly popular and there are several local clubs including one at the People's Institute, which was first established in 1865 with a reading room in a temperance hotel at 163 High Street. In 1882 the Club moved into their own premises at 1 Glasswork Street. This non-political club has no licence – alcohol is totally banned – but there are many excellent pool and snooker tables. The building was once the home of the Fleming family of which Sir Sandford Fleming is one of Kirkcaldy's greats (see Chapter Three).

The Ice Rink, now known as the Ice Arena, opened in 1938. At that time ice-skating was very popular, as was ice hockey. The Fife Flyers are still very popular and successful, having imported Canadian stars before the Second World War. There is still ice-skating, but there are also several curling clubs and in 1974 the Raith and Abbotshall Men's Team won the Edinburgh International.

Annually from 1948 there was motorbike racing in the Beveridge Park, which ceased in 1969, as the circuit was found too small and dangerous for many of the more powerful bikes. Earlier motorbike racing was on the sands.

The Town House in Kirkcaldy High Street opened in 1832 and was sold in 1935, and demolished to make way for Marks & Spencer's store. Some larger houses had to be demolished around Wemyssfield (Adelaide House and St Olafs among them) to make room for the new Town House, the building of which started before the Second World War, but was not completed until 1956.

MOTORBIKE RACING IN THE BEVERIDGE PARK 1962 KR00019

LOOKING NORTH, THE TOWN HOUSE IS SEEN ON THE RIGHT c1960 ZZZ03857

The Adam Smith Hall, opened in 1899 by Andrew Carnegie, was intended as a memorial to Adam Smith 100 years after his death. As Provost Michael Beveridge had died before his idea could be developed, it was 109 years before the hall opened. The Hall incorporated the Beveridge Library. The building was refurbished in 1974 and is now known as the Adam Smith Theatre. There are a few plays but many excellent films shown as well as local opera, Gilbert and Sullivan, and dramatic society productions as well as exhibitions and conferences. The specially written pantomime is a marvellous annual production, always with a house filled near to capacity.

In 1930, following an Act of Parliament the Royal Burgh of Dysart merged with the Royal Burgh of Kirkcaldy. In 1975 there was reorganisation when Kirkcaldy and six other burghs were combined to form one administrative unit, Kirkcaldy District. There were three district councils within Fife Regional Council. In 1996, Fife Regional Council and the three districts were combined to form one administrative area, Fife Council. This retains three similar operational areas with Kirkcaldy now a part of Central area.

In 1974, Kirkcaldy Civic Society was formed, with the aims of scrutinising all local planning applications, of recording all items of interest both in word and photographic

POSTERS OF ADAM SMITH THEATRE SHOWS ZZZ03870 and ZZZ03871

is organised, attracting over 120 people, and is very popular with local children. Doors Open Day and Scottish Archaeological Month events are also well-attended. The Society has published over 21 books and unveiled over 30 information plaques around the town.

form, and of informing people of all ages about our town. The Society has to date 160 members. The Committee organises a varied programme of events each year, including six diverse talks during the winter months and five guided walkabouts during the better weather. A popular midsummer barbeque with entertainment is held in Ravenscraig Castle. Each year a historical ghost walk

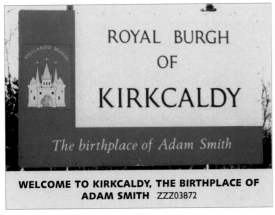

WELCOME TO KIRKCALDY, THE BIRTHPLACE OF ADAM SMITH ZZZ03872

Six of these were removed in 1996 and replaced with 'Welcome to Kirkcaldy. Twin town Ingolstadt'.

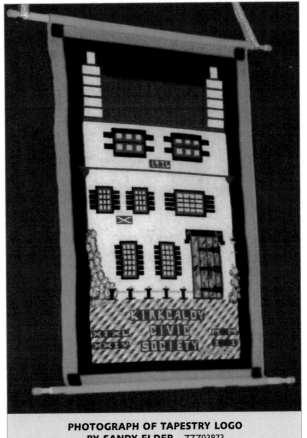

PHOTOGRAPH OF TAPESTRY LOGO BY SANDY ELDER ZZZ03873

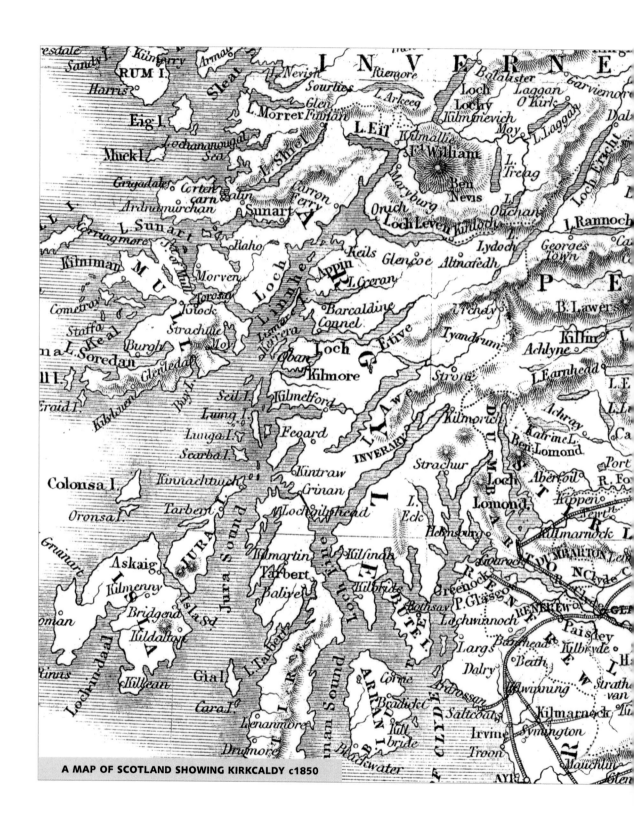

A MAP OF SCOTLAND SHOWING KIRKCALDY c1850

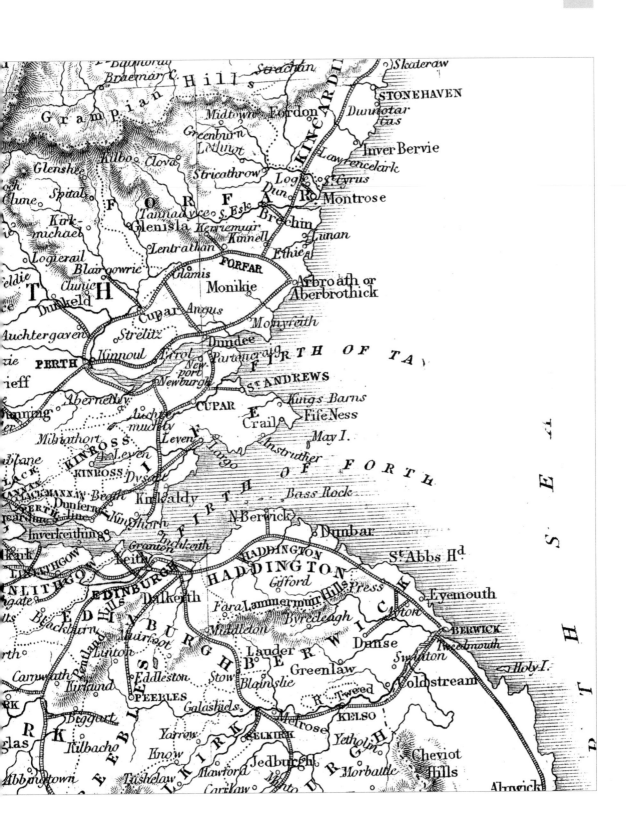

CHAPTER THREE

Greats and Personalities

ROBERT ADAM

ROBERT Adam (architect and designer, 1728–1792) was born in Gladney House, Kirkcaldy, the second son of architect William Adam who had four sons and six daughters. He attended the Burgh School before the family moved to Edinburgh in 1739, where he attended the High School. Robert then went to Edinburgh University, but he did not graduate, due to the 1745 Jacobite Rebellion. Instead, he joined his brother John as an assistant to his father. He was involved in the additions to Hopetoun House and the building of Fort George, near Nairn. Between 1754 and 1758 he went on a grand tour of Europe, mainly to Rome, where he gathered many ideas for the future. Robert then set up house in London. He was jointly appointed with William Chambers, 'Architect to the King's Works', but he relinquished this post when he became Member of Parliament for Kinross (1768–1774).

Meanwhile, he continued designing private houses, specialising in lavish exteriors and interiors, including furniture. One of the finest is Mellerstain where he rebuilt the centre block between the two wings designed by his father. Sadly, some like Mavisbank (featured on television's Restoration Programme 2003) have either been demolished or are in a poor state of repair. There were so many works commissioned in Scotland that an Edinburgh office was set up in 1772. One of these buildings was the Register House in Edinburgh. Robert Adam's major work in the capital city was Charlotte Square, which unfortunately was not completed during his lifetime. His most well-known building is probably Culzean Castle on the Ayrshire coast. This site is a very dramatic one, originally that of an ancient castle, although the present building itself is wholly classical. Robert Adam never married. He died suddenly in London in 1792, a much-revered figure.

GORDON BROWN

Gordon Brown was appointed Chancellor of the Exchequer on 2 May 1997. He has been an MP since 1983 and was Opposition spokesperson on Treasury and Economic Affairs (Shadow Chancellor) from 1992. Mr Brown was born in 1951 and was educated at West Primary School and then at Kirkcaldy High School, at which he was Dux Boy in 1967. His father, who hailed from Fife, was Minister of St Brycedale Church, Kirkcaldy from 1953 to 1967, and Gordon played for Kirkcaldy High School Rugby team, as well as Kirkcaldy Tennis Club. He went on to Edinburgh University where he gained a 1st Class Honours and then a Doctorate. He was Rector of Edinburgh University and Chairman of the University Court between 1972 and 1975. From 1976 to 1980 Mr Brown lectured at Edinburgh University, and then Caledonian University, before taking up a post at Scottish Television (1980–1983).

After becoming an MP, Mr Brown was the Chair of the Labour Party Scottish Council (1983–1984). Before becoming Shadow Chancellor he held two other senior posts on the Opposition front bench – Shadow Chief Secretary to the Treasury (1987–1989) and Shadow Trade and Industry Secretary

(1989–1992). Mr Brown has had a number of works published including 'Maxton', 'The Politics of Nationalism and Devolution' and 'Where There is Greed'. He has edited a number of books including 'John Smith: Life and Soul of the Party' and 'Values, Visions and Voices'.

Outside of work Mr Brown's interests include supporting Raith Rovers, tennis and film. He is married to Sarah. Their daughter, Jennifer, was born at Forth Park, Kirkcaldy, but died after 10 days. Their son John was born in October 2003. From May 2005, Gordon Brown is now MP for Kirkcaldy and Cowdenbeath Constituency.

MARJORIE FLEMING

Marjorie Fleming (1803–1811) was born at 130 High Street, Kirkcaldy. The three-storey house had a pend to the side, leading off from the High Street, and a garden that ran down to the sea. On the ground floor was a bookshop. Early in her short life she displayed a love of language unusual in a child so young. By the age of six she had already begun writing her own poetry and keeping her own journals. Her journals are preserved in the National Library of Scotland in Edinburgh, and Kirkcaldy Museum has a small number of her mementos. After her early death from meningitis it was nearly 50 years before anyone recorded her life. She was buried in Abbotshall Churchyard with a simple stone, 'M.F. 1803–11'. Later a marble cross was erected to 'Pet Marjorie', so named by Dr John Brown in his book 'Pet Marjorie'. In May 1930 a special stone of red granite was erected on the back of the original stone, showing Marjorie reading a

book. In 1990 Kirkcaldy Civic Society placed a plaque to her memory near the main gate of the churchyard. Kirkcaldy Civic Society, in conjunction with the Hall of Cards, has put a plaque on the house where she was born and died. From 1914 to 1920 Kirkcaldy Naturalists ran part of the building as a Marjorie Fleming Museum. Holland and Barrett now occupy the house, now numbered 132.

KIRKCALDY, MARJORIE FLEMING'S GRAVESTONE
ZZZ04412

SIR SANDFORD FLEMING

Sir Sandford Fleming (1827–1915) was born in Kirkcaldy, and educated first in Kennoway, and later at Kirkcaldy Burgh School. A qualified engineer and surveyor who had helped to lay out the railway through Kirkcaldy, he emigrated to Canada when he was 18. It was a stormy passage and thinking he would never reach his destination he wrote a farewell message to his mother, put it in a bottle and threw it into the sea. He did arrive safely and wrote to his mother. Three months later the bottle washed up on the Devon coast and the message was duly delivered to his mother.

In 1850 he founded the Canadian Journal of Literature and History. He designed the first Canadian postage stamp and pioneered the Canadian Pacific Railway, which was completed in 1885. From 1879 he campaigned for the laying of the undersea telegraph cable to connect the new and old world, that was finally laid in 1908. Time was precious to him – he pioneered the 24-hour clock and Standard Time by which to measure Local Time, which is dependent on the sun's movement. He was given the Freedom of Kirkcaldy in 1882 and was knighted in 1897. In 1973 the Archaeological and Historic Sites Board of Ontario, Canada erected a memorial plaque in Kirkcaldy War Memorial Gardens. Kirkcaldy Civic Society in 2002 unveiled a plaque at the People's Institute on the High Street/Glasswork Street corner, near his birthplace.

TOM GOURDIE MBE

Tom Gourdie's (1913–2005) main aim in life was endeavouring to improve the nation's handwriting. He visited schools for many years, instructing pupils and teachers. He had left school in his early teens, but returned and gained a scholarship to Edinburgh College of Art. In 1937 he won a £50 scholarship to visit Germany where he was introduced to Adolf Hitler (not at his request). After the war he taught at Banff and then at Kirkcaldy High School until he retired. He is also remembered for his fine intricate paintings, particularly of Fife Coalfields (his father was a miner). After retiring he lectured abroad, especially in the US, Sweden and South Africa, and was given many awards. Music was something he loved – he played both the trombone and the French horn.

Did you know?

Robert Fyfe, who attended Kirkcaldy High School where he was Dux Boy in 1948, is better known as Howard in the popular TV series 'Last of the Summer Wine'. The programme was first shown on the BBC in 1973. It was turned into a play and was taken to the stage in Eastbourne, and then Bournemouth in 1985, where Robert Fyfe appeared as a new character, Howard. Roy Clarke of BBC TV went to see the play and decided to put the character into the TV series. The rest is history.

JOHN HUNTER

John Hunter was born in Kirkcaldy in 1831, the youngest son of a local cabinetmaker and wheelwright. In time this business diversified into construction work, such as building railway stations and large villas, including Kirkcaldy Station. John was also a successful dealer in heritable property. He was active in local politics and during his lifetime was a generous benefactor to Kirkcaldy, particularly the Old Parish Church of which he was an Elder. He died in 1916, leaving his home, St Brycedale House, to the town for conversion into a hospital for the poor and incurable. The subsequent Public Trust, consisting of the Magistrates and Dean of Guild, had the remit, stipulated in the bequest, to convert the house, disburse funds to wounded soldiers and sailors, distribute any surplus among the poor and to erect a monument to John Hunter (in which he is buried standing up) in front of the house.

JOHN MACKIE

John Mackie, 'better kent as Jock' was born in Ayrshire and came to Kirkcaldy in 1930, where he worked as a confectioner for 25 years with a local firm of bakers. For 18 years he taught bakery at evening classes, winning gold medals in confectionery in Glasgow, Edinburgh and London. He then bought a small sweet shop at Carlyle Road, opposite the old Kirkcaldy High School, but pupils were banned from crossing to his shop, so at break-times he could be seen at the school wall with a tray of toffee apples, etc. He had a stall at the Links Market where he sold white and pink sugar mice and large sugary hearts. In his spare time he was a keen member of the Bowhill Burns Club. He published a small book of poems, one of which is printed below.

JOHN HUNTER (1831-1916) ZZZ03874

John Hunter, one of Kirkcaldy's benefactors who left his home for conversion into a hospital for the poor and incurable.

Arthritis

'The Hell o' a' diseases' the toothache
has been styled,
Auld Nick invented it himself
when he was but a child,
But noo since he's got aulder,
he's brocht oot a subtler pain
That wracks mankind frae end tae end
– Arthritis is the name.

And when Auld Nick tak's oot
his pipes an' plays Arthritis Reel,
The rid hot pokers up yer back
fair gaurs a buddy squeal,
While a' its close relations staun laughin' at the door,
Rheumatics, Gout, Sciatica, a' roarin' oot 'Encore'.

It's true we ha'e this Welfare State,
its panels and prescriptions,
Its Doctors' Boards and' Sick Relief
an' forms o' a' descriptions,
But when you've suffered a' ye can,
an' tried o' every caper,
Well, a' the doctor he'll gie you are
peels in silver paper.

JOHN MACKIE 1961 ZZZ03875

John Mackie was a local character – very rarely seen without his colourful headgear.

MRS MELVILLE

Mrs Melville (née Rankine) was one of the last of the Kirkcaldy pit lassies. She was born in 1828 (the same year the gallery of the parish church fell in) and lived in Sommerton Row at the top of Coal Wynd. There were no policemen at that time and two Sheriff Officers were responsible for keeping order – one for Kirkcaldy and one for the Links District. She started work at 10 years of age at the pit, which was situated at what is now Whyteman's Brae, where she was employed until she was 20. She began by helping her father to dig coal and stow his 'redd' in the waste. Her father earned about £1 a fortnight and she was paid 6d a day and from that they had to supply the oil for their lamps. Approximately a dozen pit lassies were employed, working twelve-hour shifts, six days a week and for four months of the year they never saw daylight except on Sunday.

During the first two or three years she was in the pit there was very little bad language heard until three lassies came from Kelty, and their tongues would have terrified a regiment of soldiers. Their breakfast, consisting of porridge, milk and a piece was sent down the pit at 9am Because of the extreme heat they wore very little clothing. It was really a very hard life but when the Government eventually passed a law (c1848) prohibiting women from being employed down the pit, many tears were shed by the last of the pit lassies, because there were very few jobs of any description for women, and they ended up in the mills.

DR LEWIS MOONIE

Dr Lewis Moonie has been Kirkcaldy's MP since 1987, and he was a close friend of the late John Smith. He studied medicine at St Andrews University and became a community physician. He is married with two sons and his main interests include walking, fishing, golf and bridge. During his period in Parliament he has been a junior defence minister as well as being Opposition spokesman on Broadcasting and the Media, Trade and Industry, and Science and Technology. He has always been known as an intelligent and thoughtful speaker. Dr Moonie will be standing down as an MP due to the boundary changes in Scotland. Dr Lewis Moonie has now been elevated to the peerage and is looking forward to his seat in the House of Lords.

KAREL NEKOLA

Wemyss Ware was the brainchild of Robert Heron, who owned the Fife Pottery. He based the designs on very old ware in the possession of the Wemyss family of Wemyss Castle. He needed painters to produce much brighter images of nature, so around 1880 he brought over some very talented decorators from the Continent. These included Karel Nekola (1858–1915) who had been born in Bohemia and turned out to be the Pottery's greatest asset. He was the only painter to remain here. He married, raised a family and became totally integrated into the community, having many varied interests. The family lived in Bandon Avenue, where a studio (complete with a coal-fired kiln) was built at the bottom of the garden after Nekola became partly disabled in later

life. The pottery was nearby, enabling pieces to be brought over, allowing him to decorate them. Among other organisations, he was a member of Gallatown Mutual Improvement Association. Nekola continued painting until near the end of his life. He lived in Kirkcaldy for 35 years until his death.

DISPLAY OF HERON POTTERY 2005 ZZZ03876

Heron Pottery employed Karel Nekola. (Reproduced by permission of Kirkcaldy Museum and Art Gallery)

ROBERT PHILP

Robert Philp (1751–1828) was a very successful and wealthy linen manufacturer.

Born in 1751, the eldest of a family of four, it is thought he was educated at the Burgh School, Kirkcaldy. He set out on the road supplying yarns to home weavers and later collecting the cloth they produced and selling it at fairs. Spinning and weaving became more profitable when the work was done in a factory, so he purchased the West Bridge Mills with its own bleachfield and dyeworks in the Linktown area. Robert was a very successful and wealthy linen manufacturer and became a merchant councillor and also a bailie. Although his business was in the Linktown area he attended the Old Parish Church (at that time known as St Brysse Church).

Robert Philp never married, and before he died he set up a trust with the instructions that except for a few minor bequests, all his estates were to be sold and the money invested for the education of poor children in Kirkcaldy and Kinghorn. Schools were set up in the Kirkcaldy area, but with the introduction of the Education Act of 1872 they were phased out by 1891. The only Philp school building left is on the corner of Charlotte Street and Thistle Street, which has, over the years, had many different uses, but is at present a nightclub called After Dark (AD). The trust has helped with clothing, books, etc for qualifying pupils over the years. The pupils who received help were known as 'Philpers'. The trust money still helps today, being used within the Fife Educational Trusts managed by Fife Council Education Department. Robert Philp's West Bridge Mill has recently been demolished

ROBERT PHILP (1751-1828) ZZZ03877

Robert Philp whose legacy is continuing to help local children in their education.

and the site is being used for housing.

RAITH ROVERS' GREATS

Raith Rovers introduced two of the world's greatest footballers to senior football, but the supporters' favourite players spent the majority of their careers at Stark's Park, where they were celebrated locally, rather than internationally.

No-one scored more goals for Raith Rovers than Willie Penman, a miner from Kelty, who scored 211 goals in 328 first team appearances between August 1942 and April 1954. In 1948/49, the tall, lean centre forward scored 58 goals in 47 games as Rovers won the Second Division Championship and reached the final of the Scottish League Cup. That promotion ushered in a golden period in the club's history, when they enjoyed 13 consecutive seasons in the top division, guided by manager Bert Herdman and Chairman James Gourlay.

The undoubted star of that team was left-back Willie McNaught, who then moved to centre-half to form the celebrated half-back line of Young, McNaught and Leigh. Capped five times for Scotland and six times for the Scottish League, McNaught holds the club's appearances record of 657 first team games, between 1941 and 1962.

Few have served the club longer than Johnny Urquhart, who had 10 successful years at Hearts before joining his hometown club in April 1956. He enjoyed seven successful seasons on the left wing at Stark's Park before retiring from playing to coach the youth team. He was appointed to the Board of Directors in 1965, became Chairman in 1977 and was the club's first Honorary President in 1994.

Chief amongst those who used Raith Rovers as a stepping-stone to greater things were Alex James and Jim Baxter. Both spent three years at Stark's Park during successful times for the club: James in the early 1920s, before he left for Preston North End and then Arsenal, where he was the star man in the world's best team in the mid 1930s; Baxter was sold to Rangers in 1960, and was the star of the Ibrox team that dominated Scottish football in the early 1960s. He was selected for the Rest of the World team that played at Wembley in 1963 to celebrate the Centenary of the Football Association. Like James, he started his playing career with Raith Rovers.

Did you know?

In the 18th and early 19th centuries medical schools that were desperate for bodies to be used for dissection by medical students paid body snatchers good money for fresh bodies. This led to many graveyards having Mort-houses where men kept watch on the graves of the newly buried. The only one known locally is in Abbotshall graveyard.

REVEREND ROBERT SHIRRA

Robert Shirra was born at Stirling in 1724 and at an early age was apprenticed to a tobacconist. He was deeply religious, which so impressed his employer that he provided money to help him pursue his studies for the ministry. In 1749 he was called to the vacancy at Linktown, Kirkcaldy, where he remained until 1798. He is mainly remembered for his involvement in the John Paul Jones affair. John Paul Jones, founder of the American Navy and notorious pirate, and born in Kirkbean near Kirkcubright, sailed up the Forth in 1778, threatening Kirkcaldy with bombardment. The townspeople flocked to the Reverend Shirra for help and he led them down to the shore to pray. Almost immediately, a fierce gale blew up, driving the pirate out of the Forth. The Reverend Shirra died in 1803.

ADAM SMITH

Adam Smith (1723–1790), undoubtedly the most world famous citizen of Kirkcaldy, was born in 1723 in a house close to where the main entrance of the Mercat Shopping Centre is today. His parents were Adam Smith W S, Controller of Customs and Judge Advocate for Scotland and his second wife, Margaret Douglas of Strathenry Castle, Leslie. His father died a few weeks before his birth. Adam was a delicate child – part of his illness made him absent-minded and he was often found speaking to himself. One story tells that as a four-year old, gypsies stole him. His uncle found him with the gypsies who were relieved to be rid of the squawking little boy. Adam was educated at the local Burgh School, but in 1737 at the age of 14 he attended Glasgow University and a few years later he won a Snell Scholarship to Balliol College, Oxford. During his time in Oxford he suffered bouts of poor health. He much enjoyed Balliol's excellent library but did not make many friends during his stay.

He returned to Kirkcaldy in 1746 to stay with his mother and his cousin, Jane Douglas. It was during this time he wrote his first book 'Theories of Moral Philosophy'. He was appointed Chair of Logics and Professor of Moral Philosophy at Glasgow University in 1752. He then spent the next nine years lecturing, often using examples of everyday life. His lectures were said to be very interesting. It was during this time he wrote 'The Theory of Moral Sentiments'. He became travelling tutor to the Duke of Buccleuch and travelled with him on the continent for three years, ending up for the last few months in London.

After that he returned to Kirkcaldy, living once again with his mother and cousin at 220 High Street. It was at that time he wrote the world famous 'The Wealth of Nations', published in 1776. Adam Smith was often lost in his thoughts, and early one Sunday morning he set off down his garden towards the shore in his nightclothes. When he came to, he heard the church bells ringing; he had walked to Dunfermline 12 miles along the Turnpike Road! He never married, and on his appointment as Commissioner of Customs for Scotland he moved to Edinburgh and along with his mother and cousin took up residence in Panmure House, High Street, Canongate. He founded the Oyster Club as a supper club for his friends. Three years before his death he was made Lord Rector of Edinburgh

ADAM SMITH. THIS TASSIE CAN BE SEEN IN KIRKCALDY MUSEUM AND ART GALLERY ZZZ03878

University. Adam Smith died in 1790 and is buried in Canongate Kirkyard, Edinburgh. In many countries economists make much use of Adam Smith's 'The Wealth of Nations' and both Kirkcaldy (his birthplace) and Edinburgh (where he is buried) are visited by interested groups from all over the world.

A PLAQUE IN HIS HONOUR WAS ERECTED BY THE KIRKCALDY CIVIC SOCIETY OUTSIDE THE ADAM SMITH THEATRE ZZZ03879

JOHN SMITH MD

One of Kirkcaldy's most notable medical practitioners was also a star footballer in the early years of the sport, helping to form teams in which he played, and winning Scottish Cup and FA Cup medals for Queen's Park. He played 10 times for Scotland between 1877 and 1884. Smith was described as one of the greatest Scottish forwards of the early years of the game, gifted in dribbling and shooting, superb in distribution and cool judgement. He was also a noted rugby player, and was a Scotland reserve. He was particularly tall for his day, at 6 feet 3 inches.

Having graduated MA in 1878, MB CM in 1881 and MD in 1886 from Edinburgh University, he practiced at Brycehall, Kirkcaldy (where Charles Wood's solicitors office is) for many years, a notable figure in the town as he made his house visits in a pony and trap, a black cape billowing in the breeze. Dr Smith was an honorary president of Kirkcaldy Wanderers Football Club, the town's first senior team, which played at Newton Park in what is now Ava Street. His enticement of former club Queen's Park to play a friendly match against Wanderers in Kirkcaldy did much to establish football as a spectator sport in the town.

> ## Did you know?
>
> *John Ritchie along with his brother, William, founded The Scotsman newspaper in 1817. The paper started as a weekly but by the time of John's death it had grown into a daily newspaper.*

REV T G SNODDY

The Rev T G Snoddy (1885–1971) was Minister of Pathhead Church East (now Pathhead Parish Church) from 1922 to 1958.

RAITH ROVERS c1920 ZZZ03880

In this photograph of the early 1920s Raith Rovers team, the Reverend T G Snoddy is seen second from the right in the back row.

A native of Greenock, he played football for Greenock, which helped to pay his way through college and entry to the Ministry.

In the early 1920s he also played for Raith Rovers. He was a keen walker and wrote several books about the places he walked, as well as various other topics including: 'Between Forth and Tay', 'Michael Bruce - A Biography', 'Afoot in Fife', 'Green Loanings' - Scots Verse, 'Caird Shipbuilders and J J Caird' and 'Sweetly Sang the Stars' - Verse. He was married and had three children, one of whom owned a pharmacy business in Kirkcaldy.

JOHN MCDOUALL STUART

John McDouall Stuart (1815–1866) was born in Dysart in 1815. He was one of a large family born to William Stuart and Mary McDouall from Wigtownshire. His father was appointed as Second Officer of Dysart Salt Collection, and they lived in a house just below the Rectory in Dysart (part of the dwelling has now been converted to the John McDouall Stuart Museum). After the early death of their parents the children moved to stay with relatives in Edinburgh. On finishing school John trained as a surveyor civil engineer and went to work in Glasgow.

After a broken engagement John decided to set sail to Australia. Landing in Adelaide he joined a government surveying team as a draughtsman. He took part in many expeditions but in 1858 he was commissioned to lead his own team of explorers. He embarked on six journeys which made him world famous. The two most memorable took him: firstly to the centre of Australia where he reached Alice Springs and named Mount Sturt (later to be renamed Mount Stuart); and secondly from Adelaide in the south to the Indian Ocean, Van Dieman Gulf near Darwin in the north and return – a journey of 4,000 miles. Although all members of his expedition survived the hazards of the journey McDouall Stuart fell ill, and had to be carried the last 700 miles, slung between two horses on a makeshift ambulance. He received many accolades and grants of money. He returned to London in 1864 and died two years later. He is buried in Kensal Green Cemetery, London. In Australia there is an international John McDouall Stuart Society with links to Scotland, England and Canada.

JOHN MCDOUALL STUART'S BIRTHPLACE, WHICH NOW HOUSES A MUSEUM IN HIS HONOUR ZZZ03881

A BEAUTIFUL STAINED GLASS WINDOW, WHICH IS SITUATED IN THE ABC CINEMA 2005 ZZZ03882

JOHN D SWANSON

John D Swanson was born in 1875 and became a town councillor and an architect. He was in partnership with William Williamson. They designed many fine theatres including the Palace Theatre and the King's Theatre, both in Kirkcaldy. Both these theatres later became cinemas. The Palace Theatre was gutted by fire in 1945. The King's Theatre had a sumptuous interior, supposedly based on the much larger King's Theatre in Edinburgh. It was known latterly as the ABC Cinema and has been lying empty for a few years. John D Swanson's son was a well-respected general practitioner in Kirkcaldy for many years. The photograph shown was taken after the cinema closed. The window had been hidden from the public view for many years.

JOCKY WILSON

Jocky Wilson was born in 1951 and worked as a miner in Seafield Colliery. While unemployed he won Butlin's Grand Masters Darts Competition in 1979, which came with a prize of £500. Jocky then shot up the world rankings in darts, reaching the top eight by the end of the year. In 1982 millions of TV viewers witnessed Jocky defeat John Lowe to lift the Embassy World Professional Championship Trophy – the first Scot to do so. He made a comeback in 1989 when he became World Champion again after suffering a slight drop in form in the middle of the decade. Latterly he has been honoured in the Darts Hall of Fame, which is based in Martinsburgh, West Virginia, USA. He currently lives in Kirkcaldy.

Victoria Cross

Two Kirkcaldy men have been awarded the Victoria Cross.

Lieutenant-Colonel W T Marshall VC, 19th Hussars

In the Sudan War (1882–84) W T Marshall (1885–1920), by then a quartermaster, having risen from the ranks, rescued his general who had been severely wounded when his horse was shot from under him, and took him back to the British lines. Lieutenant-Colonel Marshall is buried in Kirkcaldy's Bennochy cemetery and a wreath is laid on his grave every year.

THE IMPRESSIVE GRAVESTONE OF LIEUTENANT-COLONEL W T MARSHALL 2005 KI97707k

Private Robert Dunsire VC

During the First World War Robert was awarded a Victoria Cross for rescuing comrades wounded by enemy fire and bringing them back safely. He returned home to receive his award but was sadly killed on his next tour of duty in 1915. As Robert had been a pupil at Pathhead Primary School and he was married and lived in Buckhaven his name appears on both Kirkcaldy and Buckhaven and Methil War Memorials.

Private Robert Dunsire, V.C.
(Photo: Fife Council Museums: Methil Heritage Centre)

PRIVATE ROBERT DUNSIRE VC c1915 ZZZ03883
(Photograph courtesy of Fife Council Museum, Methil Heritage Centre)

JOCKY WILSON 1982 ZZZ03884

Jocky Wilson in a jubilant mood holding aloft his well earned 1982 Embassy World Professional Championship Trophy.

Did you know?

In the early 19th century miners and their families lived in houses owned by the coal owners and did not have to pay rent or taxes. They only had to pay the hewing price for their coal. People were healthier but if they took ill the colliery doctor treated them. Every year doctors visited the Row and as well as supplying medicine gave beer to the men and apples to the women and children. One woman who was given a supply of (bi)carbonate of soda found out it was good for baking bannocks and soon there was a great run on the soda before the doctor found out what it was being used for. There was little schooling as children went to work from an early age.

GEORGE LOWRIE

George Lowrie was the major manufacturer of clay pipes in Kirkcaldy at the turn of the century. In 1895 he and his brother William were then established at 58 Cowan Street, where the swimming pool is today. By 1906 the firm had moved to 13 Sands Road, now the Esplanade. The house was called Marine Cottage (demolished). The workshops with kiln were across the garden. White pipe clay was imported from Cornwall and stored in the basement of the cottage. There were at least four employees and production was varied. Pipes were shaped in metal moulds, which produced decoration on the pipe bowl.

The pipe maker's name and the customer's name could also be impressed before firing the pipes in a kiln. Many of Lowrie's pipes were made for pubs or tobacconists in the

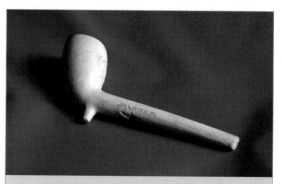

THIS PHOTOGRAPH SHOWS AN EXAMPLE OF A LOWRIE PIPE ZZZ03885

Andrew Wilson

Andrew Wilson was a Baxter or baker whose bakery was in Flesh Wynd, Pathhead, Kirkcaldy. He had the reputation of being a smuggler. Along with his friend Andrew Robertson he decided to rob a Customs Officer in Pittenweem. Unfortunately they killed him. They were soon apprehended and sent for trial to Edinburgh in 1736. Both were condemned to death by hanging. On the Sunday before the hanging Wilson and Robertson attended church and while Wilson caused a diversion Robertson escaped. Wilson was unable to follow him and was hanged in the Grassmarket. The spectators attacked the guards, so Captain Porteous ordered the soldiers to fire into the crowd and a number of people were killed. Captain Porteous was sent for trial and although found guilty he was reprieved. The mob was so angry they broke into his quarters, dragged him out into the Grassmarket and hanged him from a distaff. Andrew Wilson's grave is in the Pathhead Feuars' graveyard, Kirkcaldy. A stone erected by public subscription marks his grave, and the Porteous Riots have entered folklore.

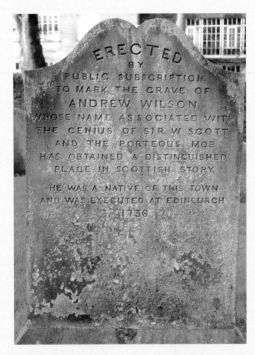

ANDREW WILSON'S GRAVESTONE 2005 KR00020
This gravestone to Andrew Wilson is in Pathhead Feuars' graveyard and was paid for by public subscription.

Kirkcaldy area and marked with their name. Pipes were delivered by horse and cart. The firm closed when George Lowrie died in 1915. When George died, his brother William was at sea with the Navy, and he never returned to Kirkcaldy.

SANDY WATSON

Between 222 and 224 High Street, Kirkcaldy is Adam Smith's Close. This is a long and narrow passageway leading to the Esplanade, with high white walls and a single streetlight. Around 1930, Sandy Watson, who was Town Officer, but had formerly been a policeman, boasted that he could win any race provided he chose the venue and could have a one-yard start. His challenger was dismayed to find the course chosen was Adam Smith's Close, so narrow that he could not squeeze past the large Town Officer!

THE LAST TRAIN FROM SINCLAIRTOWN STATION ZZZ03886

How many got on this train without paying?

SANDY WATSON'S RACE c1930
GUESS WHO CAME IN SECOND?
ZZZ03887 (Sketch by Mary Frew)

Centenary of St. Peter's Church
Congregation re-established 1811.

IN CONNECTION WITH THE PAGEANT

✷ A BAZAAR ✷

In aid of Church Funds, will be held in

DYSART PARK

ON

Wednesday, June 28th, & Saturday, July 1st

FROM 3 TO 8 P.M.

◈ STALLS ◈

FANCY WORK (1)—Dunnikier & Balbirnie—
The Misses Oswald and the Misses Balfour.
(2)—Rectory—
Mrs WARING, Mrs SMITH, Mrs LUMSDEN.

Foreign Ware—   *Art & Pottery—*   *Household Goods—*
Mrs MICHAEL NAIRN,   Mrs TOD and   Mrs LENDRUM
Mrs G. BEVERIDGE.   Mrs J. DIXON.

Sweets—
Mrs SCOTT and Mrs STEWART SMITH.

TEAS will also be served on the Grounds,   -   Price 1/-, and 6d.
There will also be a CAKE AND LEMONADE STALL

PAGEANT TICKETS ADMIT TO THE BAZAAR.

ON SUNDAY, JULY 2nd—

Special Centenary Services

WILL BE HELD IN ST PETER'S CHURCH.

Preacher at 11.30 and 6.30—
The Most Rev. THE LORD PRIMUS of the Scottish Episcopal Church.
Most Rev. W. J. F. ROBBERDS, D.D.

A POSTER FOR A BAZAAR IN
DYSART PARK   ZZZ03888

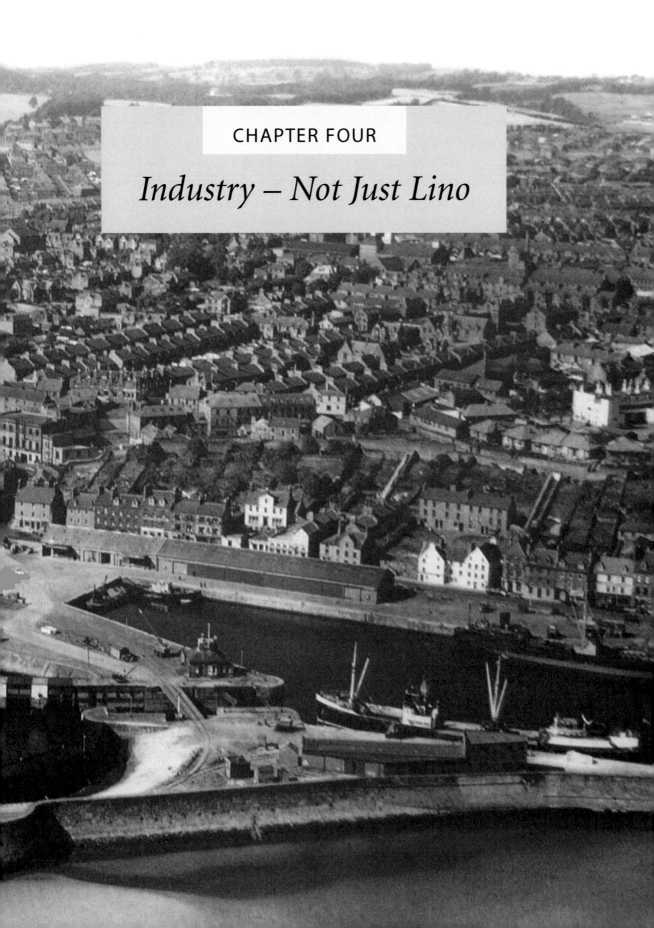

CHAPTER FOUR

Industry – Not Just Lino

'FOR I KEN MASEL' by the queer-like smell that the next stop's Kirkcaddy'. So wrote the young Miss Mary Edgar (later Mary Campbell Smith) of Merchiston School in Edinburgh in her famed 1913 poem 'The Boy in the Train'. The butt of many jokes, the characteristic but not unpleasant smell of boiling linseed oil was synonymous with the linoleum industry and with Kirkcaldy, which by then had become the undisputed linoleum capital of the world. This environmentally friendly product is still made locally, and readers can see the whole poem displayed at Kirkcaldy railway station – cut in linoleum by

computer! But this industry - which for over half a century was vast for the size of the town – was the outcome of earlier centuries of textile production largely based on imported flax, which created among other products sailcloth, floorcloth, carpets and fine linens. Coal, salt, malt, pottery and printing were also among the local industries.

The collapse of these industries, which hit Kirkcaldy particularly hard in the mid 20th century, led to attempts by the then Town Council to bring in new work opportunities. For 40 years hydraulic pumps were manufactured, there was a successful

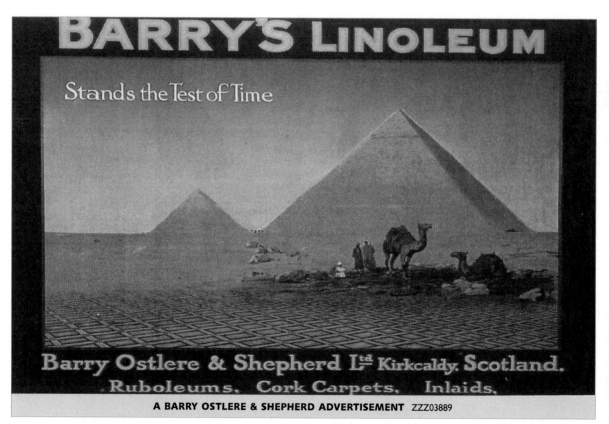

A BARRY OSTLERE & SHEPHERD ADVERTISEMENT ZZZ03889

A Barry Ostlere & Shepherd advertisement invoking the Pyramids: unfortunately it was not this firm – whose works have now all vanished – which ultimately stood the test of time, but Nairn (now Forbo-Nairn).

BUCKET PATTS KR00021

A Victorian view of the Bucket Patts, a pool from which seawater was dipped to replenish saltpans at low tide; the salt industry is long extinct and the pool now lies beneath the 1920s sea wall.

children's clothing industry, and even more jobs flourished for a few decades in the making of telephone exchange equipment. For a time metal buildings were fabricated, and more recently huge aerogenerator blades were made.

But most of these attempts to introduce a steady basis of local employment eventually foundered, and what was once a highly prosperous industrial town has sadly few significant local industries postdating 1970. Because re-equipment of the various surviving industries has repeatedly cut their workforces, for the past quarter century Kirkcaldy has been regrettably prominent in unemployment terms. This chapter cannot mention all the firms or sites involved in Kirkcaldy's very varied industrial history, but by grouping the major local industries and mentioning key interrelationships we can see how they grew, thrived and in too many cases declined.

SEAFARING AND HARBOURS

At a time when blocks of flats are springing up around its almost vacant harbour, Kirkcaldy may not appear to have been much of a seafaring centre. But it was as a commercial port, based on coastal, North Sea and Baltic

A VIEW OF KIRKCALDY HARBOUR AND THE SOUTHWEST c1960 ZZZ03855

trade in coal, grain, timber and flax, that the town had its first flowering. Most local industries used Kirkcaldy harbour, which continued to be improved until a century ago. Meantime the little harbour of its historic neighbour Dysart grew mainly as a coal port, also importing Devon clay for the Fife Pottery, until its commerce failed in 1929. Since then the increasing size of ships, the growth in road haulage and the large number of alternative ports around the Firth of Forth where better facilities could readily be developed, led to a cessation of growth at Kirkcaldy harbour. Its long sad decline ended with its closure as a commercial port in 1992.

Did you know?

Kirkcaldy was a port rather than a livestock market, but tanning was recorded in Dysart by 1330. At Pathhead – long famous for 'Meal and Malt' – maltings still work, and flour is milled at East Bridge. A butter industry that moved into the Randolph estate a generation ago remains active, and bacon is still cured in a Dysart factory, but mail is now sorted on the site of the mid 20th-century abattoir at Oriel Road.

GRAIN

Though Kirkcaldy's once-thriving corn market vanished around 1880, the central belt of Scotland provided a ready market for flour from Kirkcaldy's mills; a great millstone from a former mill in Bennochy Road came to light in 2005. The surviving East Bridge mills still supply many bakeries and the sadly threatened maltings at Overton Road (threatened closure December 2005), formerly Kilgour's, still contribute malt to many Scotch whisky distilleries. For a time there was also distilling at East Bridge, and micro brewing is still carried on in a local pub.

ANIMAL PRODUCTS

Fife is not a livestock-intensive area, except nowadays for chickens, and farm animals may never have been marketed in Kirkcaldy in any great numbers, but tanning – locally now defunct – was evidently an industry in Dysart as early as 1330. Bacon has long been cured in a small factory in Dysart and also now at nearby Auchtertool, and a butter industry, which moved into the town's Randolph estate a generation ago also remains active. Throughout the mid 20th century livestock were slaughtered on an industrial scale at Oriel Road; the Royal Mail now sorts the post on the site.

QUARRYING

Until the early 20th century Kirkcaldy was largely built of locally quarried stone. The vertical face of the medieval quarry at Dysart harbour remains in evidence, and southwest of Invertiel can still be seen some vestiges of Mr Birrell's shallow quarry. But these are almost the only signs of an industry that at one time had multiple sites, for there were once stone quarries at Coal Wynd, Sauchenbush, Southerton and a deep limestone quarry east of Chapel village. Most were infilled in the late 20th century, not necessarily with solid material safe for building on. The valley of the Den Burn west of Forbo-Nairn's linoleum factory was casually infilled with any material that came to hand; this explains why the area is now used for playing fields.

EARLY COALMINING

The opening of local collieries, literally just trenches in the ground where outcrop coal was dug out, probably began under the supervision of the monks. Dunfermline's great abbey controlled Kirkcaldy from 1075 and soon established an outpost at Abbotshall. By c1200, such workings probably existed in the Links area to the south, and later grew along the crest and slopes of the hills to the north, and wherever coal outcropped throughout the town. After the outcrop coal had been removed, bell pits were opened, in which from a hole cut in the overburden rock, ladders led down to a coal seam from which extraction took place until safety considerations – or unheralded collapses, which took the lives of the few people working there – led to abandonment.

Another way of working was to dig adits or tunnels leading up from the harbours, providing access, drainage and a means of export; the mouth of one such tunnel can still be seen at the head of Dysart harbour, where the main coal seam, some 8 metres thick, was exploited by 1330 and in earnest from 1407. From these coastal tunnels – there is another at West Wemyss – more extensive underground workings were developed on the 'stoop and room' system (known in England as 'pillar and stall') which like the earlier bell pits left the future stability of the ground above to chance. It is said that cows have vanished into old bell pits in the Gallatown area, and buildings still occasionally crack as uncharted mine workings settle.

Inland workings later developed through

using horse-worked 'gins', effectively capstans. Such ropes were made in Kirkcaldy, both in the Den area and from 1843 at Invertiel, serving both this need and the maritime market; string for domestic purposes was also made. The small Pannie Pit (Dunnikier

GATHERING SEA COAL c1935 KR00022

Did you know?

Steam engines were used at Dysart by 1764 to pump water from coal pits, and later for winding coal and men with locally made hemp ropes. Starting in 1855 – making guns for the Crimean War – Douglas & Grant of Den Road became a major maker of colliery winding engines, including Scotland's deepest pit, the Mary at Lochgelly. In the First World War they made capstans for the Navy, but the General Strike of 1926 sealed their doom.

small pits near the heart of the town, accessed from comparatively shallow vertical shafts, up which coal, 'blaes' and 'redd' (waste rock) and the miners themselves were lifted by rope,

Colliery), open in 1894, had only two rail sidings, both short; its site has been recycled – for recycling uses! At Dysart, adjacent to the conserved Pan Ha' whose name derives from the salt panning industry, was the small Lady Blanche colliery, closed in 1928. The rotting timbers then used to support the covering of its fortunately shallow pit shaft collapsed in the 1980s, while the risk of continuing instability of the ground above the heavily worked Dysart main seam is the reason for the Randolph playing fields.

This evocative picture shows the gathering of sea coal in the early 20th century; this may have come from outcrops, or from waste tipping on the beach at Dysart.

HIDDEN LEGACIES OF MINING

In the early 1970s Fife County Council decided to build a reception centre for children coming into care at the top of Whyteman's Brae, an area known to be unstable from early 19th century mining. Boreholes failed to reveal the extreme extent of honeycombing, and the concrete grout that was pumped into the ground found its unseen way downhill to emerge from old adits at the Port Brae. So the project was moved to Glenrothes and the undermined site abandoned – it remains open ground to this day. Similar concerns also influenced the decision taken around 1975 to recondition rather than replace the Glebe Park housing.

PINS AND PROPELLER SHAFTS

Local metal industries followed from coalmining, and from the relatively brief exploitation of a little ironstone found in central Fife. The earliest products included pins and nails, made by 1724 in Dysart parish. This included Pathhead, where pioneer economist Adam Smith used the pin factory as an exemplar in his influential work, 'The Wealth of Nations'. Its whereabouts are now unknown, but a successor industry, the Fife Forge at Pathhead, transformed ingots cast at Parkhead in Glasgow into such major items as ships' propeller shafts, an activity that sadly died in 1984 with much of the European shipbuilding industry.

DEEP PITS, WINDING ENGINES AND SCRAP METAL

Meantime steam engines – used at Dysart by 1764 – had been introduced to pump water from the ever-deepening coal pits, and later for winding coal and men with hemp ropes, and ultimately steel cables. For a time steel pipes were made on the site where Kirkcaldy fire station now stands. From 1845 Lewis Grant worked in Dysart, making rice machinery, and a decade ago moved to Mitchelston to produce computer casings from sheet metal. Meantime from a small start in 1855, making guns for the Crimean War, Douglas & Grant of Den Road became a major maker of steam winding engines for collieries, including Scotland's deepest, the Mary pit at Lochgelly. In the First World War they made capstans for the Navy, but the General Strike of 1926 sealed their doom and the former rail connected site, like that of the Fife Forge, is now a scrapyard. In fact with the decline of local heavy industry and the growth of the all-steel car, vehicle dismantling and scrap metal recovery has been a major and too-prominent feature of Kirkcaldy for four decades: small wonder that more cars cross the Forth Road Bridge northwards than ever return south!

IRONFOUNDING AND COPPER CYLINDERS

Meantime in the late 19th century ironfounding had developed locally: Mackie cast primitive mangles under the brash trade name of 'Globe Champion'! Their crudity may have caused the firm's failure, but John Bryce's successful foundry at Dunnikier Road later incorporated boiler-making. The town's final cast iron products were manhole covers of a particular Kirkcaldy pattern. These were specified for the rapid and extensive development of council housing in the 1950s and 1960s, both around the old town to remedy its appalling housing conditions, and a few miles to the north to house the growing population of Glenrothes; the last foundry – John Leitch – which also used brass, closed c1985. House-building may also have led to the local manufacture – not long ceased – of copper cylinders for domestic hot water.

FROM DEEP PITS TO OPENCASTING

The once large Randolph Colliery north of Boreland was rail-connected until it closed in 1968, but the old and deep Frances Colliery survived on the Dysart cliff top, its coal always leaving by rail in primitive loose-coupled open trucks, crossing Normand Road on the level. The pit wastes were irresponsibly tipped down the Dubbie Braes into the sea, to be swept along by waves and tides, infilling Dysart harbour with silt, and ruining Kirkcaldy Sands. Eventually a tunnel linked the Frances Colliery with the vast Seafield Colliery south of the town, sunk in the 1950s by the NCB (National Coal Board) on the site of a smaller enterprise.

SEAFIELD COLLIERY 1977 KR00023

This shows Seafield Colliery as seen from a railway train in 1977, with the lorry loading point on the left and rusty 16-ton rail wagons on the right; by then most coal left by rail in modern hopper wagons.

Seafield's 2,000 workers were in fact mainly employed beneath the sea; those wastes that could not be stowed in worked-out undersea areas were taken by road to infill a small valley at Kilrie beside the Bernard's Smithy road (now the B9157). The coal was mainly taken to power stations by rail, at first in the same way as at Frances Colliery; but the extensive sidings later became largely redundant with the introduction of long trains of hopper wagons. The rail crossover, which gave access to the colliery from the south, came in very handy for single-line working when a coastal landslip at nearby Abden threatened the closure of the East Coast Main Line.

The great complex was closed abruptly in 1988 as a result of the disastrous confrontation between the would-be immovable mass of the National Union of Mineworkers and the – for a time – unstoppable force of the Thatcher government. Seafield's pair of tall winding towers, prominent reminders of this absurd collision of rival dogmas, were each spectacularly demolished in a few seconds in 1989. The two shafts were capped, and the abandoned and cleared pithead area is now fast turning from brownfield to private housing, the southern areas regraded to give the new owners the chance of seaward views.

Across the town the gaunt pithead gear of the former Frances Colliery still stands, conserved just after the Millennium as a

THE FRANCES COLLIERY 2005 K197709k

Old and new: the finely reconditioned headgear of the Frances Colliery is seen here, with 21st century industrial buildings on the left.

monument to this once great industry, whose passing led to much trauma in Fife, as in other mining communities across Britain. Part of the Frances Colliery site has however been recently redeveloped for industry and become the new home of the Carlton Bakery of Kirkcaldy.

Coal's latest manifestation is in the yawning opencast workings that currently flank the northern slopes of the hills on which Boreland, Mitchelston and the Central Fife Retail Park now stand; the last vestiges of the once prominent 'bing' or waste heap of the Randolph pit were removed in the early years of the 21st century in a major opencasting job.

LINEN

There is no record of the start of the local spinning and weaving of flax fibres into linens before 1715, when Mr Millie officially began spinning in Dysart, but it was probably carried on earlier in a small way, and was to become the town's most extensively practised trade, being appropriate to handwork as well as capable of intensive mechanisation. By 1748 the Arnots organised the hand weaving of linens at Pathhead, and by c1765 there was a dyeworks in central Kirkcaldy. John Fergus from Newburgh became a well-known local linen manufacturer; streets of villas are named after him. A bleachworks was busy at Abbotshall by 1792, and the Ninian

LOCKHART'S LINEN FACTORY ZZZ03890

The front building of Lockhart's linen factory in Links Street still stands as shops and flats.

Lockharts had weaving sheds at the north end of Linktown by 1797. Gallatown was a hand-weaving centre by 1799, and from 1806 flax was spun by waterpower at the West Mill; the now drained Mill Dam was probably built about then to store the water of the Tiel Burn against dry periods.

By 1822 Aytoun was running tow mills in Nicol Street, and two years later Ingram had a bleachfield at East Bridge. Dysart flax spinning had intensified by 1827, by which time Lumsden had developed the Denburn bleachfield. The famous name of Nairn, virtually synonymous with Kirkcaldy until the late 20th century, entered the town's record in 1828 with the opening of Michael Nairn's first canvas factory at Coal Wynd. Four years later there were jute mills in the town, though Dundee was to dominate this particular aspect of textiles; in 1855 the West Bridge Mills were built on a grand scale to a Dundee pattern. By 1864 the linen industry was very widespread in Fife, providing nearly 1,500 jobs in the town; Aytoun, Hendry, Malcolm and Swan were power spinners, while John Jeffrey and Robert Wemyss were power weavers. Later in the century Beveridge too made linens, and became a great philanthropist for the town.

The industry then began a long decline. In the later 20th century many mills were

PHILP'S OLD MILL NEAR THE WEST BRIDGE c2000 KR00024

Philp's old mill near the West Bridge is seen here shortly before demolition c2000; the floodlights of Stark's Park appear above.

BLYTH'S HAWKLYMUIR FACTORY 1991 KR00025

This shows Blyth's Hawklymuir factory, a Gallatown linen works which closed in 1960 and has since been used for storage by successive local authorities.

demolished, but the former Hawklymuir factory of Blyth at Gallatown, closed in 1960, has since been used for storage, and Robert Stocks's mill in the Links, which closed about 1973, soon became a retail carpet warehouse. The nearby West Bridge Mills, long derelict, were reconditioned in 1995 for social use.

The stone footings of the tall Lockhart mill that closed in 1984 can still be seen under the garages of the Abbots Mill flats fronting Abbotshall Road, and Halley's house and office still stand in Nicol Street, the attached dyeworks site now also strikingly redeveloped for flats. The last textiles survivor, the Victoria linen mills of 1854 – enlarged over the years – still work at Sinclairtown.

THE RESTORED WEST BRIDGE MILLS, WHICH OPENED AS THE FOYER IN 1995 KI97710k

THE VICTORIA LINEN MILLS, SINCLAIRTOWN 2005 K197713k

First built in 1854, they were repeatedly extended up to the 1970s and are still in operation.

FLOORCLOTH

Floorcloth originated in England in the 1820s as crudely painted linen, but in 1847 canvas manufacturer Michael Nairn, believing he could do better, built his famous 'Folly' on the top of a former sea cliff at Pathhead, importing skilled workers from England and developing the manufacturing process. Nairns held a monopoly of floorcloth production in Scotland until 1866 when Shepherd and

Beveridge left to start their own works at Factory Road, and by 1879 their National Floorcloth Works stood at Bennochy Bridge on the site now occupied by Carlyle House.

In 1869 Nairn opened a new canvas factory beside Kirkcaldy harbour. He was still leading the floorcloth trade, and industrial journalist of *The Scotsman*, David Bremner, described in flowery detail his remarkable plant built into the steep hillside. The weaving of the coarse

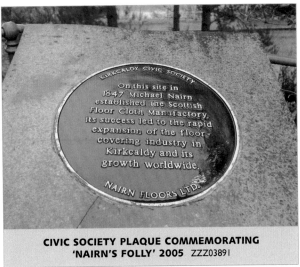

CIVIC SOCIETY PLAQUE COMMEMORATING 'NAIRN'S FOLLY' 2005 ZZZ03891

The Civic Society Plaque commemorating 'Nairn's Folly', the Scottish Floorcloth Manufactory; the Society has now provided over 30 commemorative plaques around the town.

Folly was demolished c1970, and its steep site overlooking the Forth was soon laid out as public gardens by the energetic but ill-fated Town Council.

LINOLEUM, BOUNCING BOMBS AND VINYL FLOOR COVERINGS

Linoleum was invented in England in 1860 by Frederick Walton; his process used a mixture of finely ground cork, wood flour and the linseed oil that gave its name, applied to a hessian or jute backing. Walton's patent expired in 1876, and in 1877 the Nairn company added 'lino', as it became called, to their floorcloth specialism. In 1879 they built the world's first lino factory, a tall stone edifice, which, while internally rebuilt many years ago, still stands long-derelict and unloved at Pathhead, awaiting the now hopeful outcome

flax base, and the alternate sizing by brush and the application of thick paint to the cloth by trowel were still handworked. So was the pattern printing operation, which applied mock marbling, wood or chintz effects using blocks; this followed months of drying the painted cloth in warm air, heated and blown by one of two steam engines, which also drove mills making 20 tons of paint a week, and used steam to boil linseed oil. Nairn's

of lengthy negotiations for reuse. Meantime Nairns had crossed under the railway line to expand inland, and developed major interests in the USA and Australia.

While lino production was suspended during the Second World War the huge Nairn factory made a multiplicity of war materials, the most memorable being the casings for Barnes Wallis's bouncing bombs. Many other lino factories were built by competing firms in the early 20th century, the greatest being west of Kirkcaldy station, owned by Barry Ostlere & Shepherd (BOS, latterly Barry Staines). BOS closed in 1964 and most of their buildings were soon demolished. The Forth Avenue sites became public gardens in the 1970s, the remainder being developed in the 1980s for the Fife College of Nursing and Midwifery, now an outpost of Dundee University. One of the earliest BOS buildings

THE COMPLEX OF BARRY OSTLERE & SHEPHERD FACTORIES AT FORTH AVENUE c1950 KR00027

To the right at the rear are the old railway station, the Art Gallery, Technical College and the spire of St Brycedale's Church.

survived in Junction Road as Meiklejohn's golf caddy cart factory until the 1990s, the site being cleared and intensively redeveloped for flats in 2004–05.

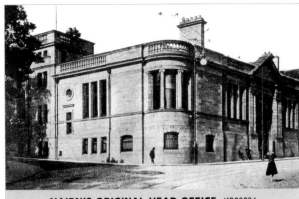

NAIRN'S ORIGINAL HEAD OFFICE KR00026

Nairn's original head office was adjacent to Path House; it was superseded in the 1950s by Braehead House, now flats. This attractive red sandstone building was sadly demolished about 1972.

Linoleum was for decades block-printed like floorcloth, but was later expensively inlaid by hand or cheaply machine printed. After 1945 some was cut into tiles, and Nairns soon turned to making vinyl tiles, surviving the collapse of the lino cartel by merging with Williamson of Lancaster in 1962; a decade later the factory still employed about 2,000. From 1975 owned by the palm-oil giant Unilever, the plant was sold on in 1986 to rival floor covering manufacturers Forbo

NAIRN FLOORING ADVERT 1984 ZZZ03892
(Reproduced by courtesy of the Forbo-Nairn archivist)

Colourful draft advertisement for a Nairn flooring product in 1984; but while linoleum output is to continue, the Forbo-Nairn vinyl floor covering production is about to cease.

of Switzerland. From c1990 their lino has been cut by computer-controlled water jets into the most intricate of patterns - *vide* the poem at the railway station - though these do require reassembly by hand. Forbo-Nairn have retained a very substantial plant to make lino in sheet form, but due to the rise in popularity of laminated floorings their modern factory producing 'Cushionflor', a 4-metre wide vinyl sheet floor covering with foam backing, which thrived into the early 21st century, now faces early closure and the loss of 110 jobs. This will leave Forbo-Nairn with little more than one-tenth of Nairn's 1972 workforce.

CARPETS AND CHILDREN'S CLOTHING

Victoria Carpets worked in Kirkcaldy for a decade before moving to Kiddermister in 1901. James Meikle developed dyeing and carpet making in Dysart from 1919, and his firm moved their weaving operations in 1956 to the former Wemyss's Caledonian linen mill of 1898 at Balsusney, soon employing 600 people. Meikles sadly closed in 1980, their sites soon being redeveloped for housing. Babygro arrived in the 1960s as a maker of children's clothing, and at one time had other Fife branches, but its extensive Hayfield factory recently closed.

PRINTING

In 1838 The Fifeshire Advertiser newspaper was founded in Kirkcaldy, and in 1867 expanded from general printing into lithography, with the aid of Archibald Beveridge from West Wemyss, who had trained in Edinburgh. Beveridge set up in business on his own in 1869, soon moving on from hand presses to the faster cylinder type, producing illustrated catalogues of linoleum patterns and providing general and specialist printing services to local industries; his men were soon working in several buildings. One was on the site where the Fife Free Press office now stands; under Strachan & Livingston this less historic paper later absorbed The Advertiser and – reaching a peak in the 1960s – opened a centralised printing plant at Mitchelston where a whole series of local newspapers were rolled off, though the loss of local control eventually caused this latter activity to be moved away to Falkirk in the millennium year.

Meantime, in 1877 Beveridge had built a factory in Church Lane at the rear of the Old Kirk; it was there that a fine large-scale map series covering Kirkcaldy Burgh was lithographed for the council in 1880 – a set is still held in the Forbo-Nairn archives. When Beveridge died in 1892 his manager, J H Allen, took over and although the original factory burned down in 1900, it was quickly rebuilt and then successively enlarged in 10 stages up to 1938 under the Allen dynasty. The firm at first relied heavily on the production of pattern books for the growing linoleum industry, but successfully served many markets including printing chocolate wrappers, seed packets and colour calendars. As 'Allen Litho' it bought a small Markinch printing firm and stayed independent up until 1988. Its successor firm, Inglis Allen of Falkirk, still has its Kirkcaldy plant on

A SKETCH OF ARCHIBALD BEVERIDGE'S FIRST PRINTING WORKS IN REDBURN WYND ZZZ03893

the site. The last Allen connected with the works wrote an excellent history of the firm, published in 1998. Multiprint, established c1980, still has its modern plant in Seafield Road (see ZZZ04413, below).

THE MULTIPRINT PAIR OF MODERN PRINTING WORKS AT SEAFIELD ROAD 2005 ZZZ04413

SALT, TEAPOTS AND CERAMIC CATS

From medieval times slack coal was burned to evaporate seawater in iron pans to make sea salt, a noted local activity on various coastal sites until superseded by rock salt in the early

20th century. Coal also fired bricks, made in the Denburn valley by 1728 and up until the late 19th century. Pottery was made in Linktown as early as 1714, using local coal, and clay from a pit where Balwearie High School now stands – hence the tiny arch under the railway, built in 1847 to allow the tramway to continue to carry tubs of clay down to the pottery at Methven Street (named after the firm). The Fife Pottery worked at Gallatown from 1790, lending its name to Pottery Street and later

BALWEARIE UPPER MILL c1980 KR00028

An old waterwheel at Balwearie Upper Mill c1980, which once drove flint-grinding machinery. A restored Kirkcaldy waterwheel now turns at the conservation village of New Lanark.

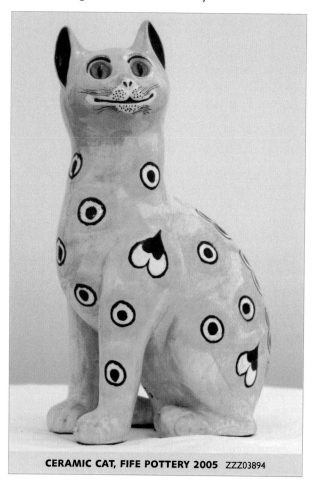

CERAMIC CAT, FIFE POTTERY 2005 ZZZ03894

A restored ceramic cat from the Fife Pottery; reproductions of Wemyss Ware are still made in Fife.

becoming well-known for its 'Wemyss Ware' and its whimsical and colourful ceramic cats, using Devon clay. Flint was ground for local potteries in water mills at Balwearie.

Two new potteries opened in Sinclairtown, in 1869 and 1879, though the first - MacLauchlan's – which made teapots, bowls and dishes, closed in 1899. All the remaining local potteries were extinguished by the great depression around 1930. Though their distinctive bottle kilns have vanished, the great wheel from one flint mill now turns at New Lanark, as the sole relic of a once significant Kirkcaldy industry. However, the famous cats have for some years been reproduced in Ceres by Griselda Hill. Fireplace making may be thought of as being entirely a sunset industry, but it still carries on locally and has even taken an expanding share of a shrinking market.

FURNITURE FOR QUEENS AND SCHOOLKIDS

A local tradition of building small ships in timber at Dysart was active until a century ago, but the shipyard by Kirkcaldy harbour faded after 1865 when the local marine engineering firm of Key decided to build iron ships at the nearby burgh of Kinghorn. But cabinetmaking grew, and by 1879 A H McIntosh was making furniture for shipbuilders, establishing a plant at Victoria Road. His house, later built alongside, is now the heart of the Victoria Hotel. This firm fitted and furnished the increasingly palatial Atlantic liners of the early and mid 20th century, largely Clyde-built and including the 'Queen Mary' and her ill-fated sister ship, the 'Queen Elizabeth', which was later intended as a conference centre and sank off Hong Kong.

THE MCINTOSH FURNITURE FACTORY   KR00029

The McIntosh furniture factory in Victoria Road is seen here in Edwardian days. The Kirkcaldy trams were narrow and ran on narrow-gauge tracks until closure in 1931. The factory burned down in 1969 and the firm moved out to Mitchelston with Town Council assistance.

KIRKCALDY, THE ESA McINTOSH FACTORY 2005 ZZZ04414

The ESA McIntosh factory, which moved to this site in 1970.

McIntosh had by then established itself in the top end of the domestic furniture market, and in 1970 moved into a fine new factory at Mitchelston, though many subsequent ups and downs led to a takeover by school desk makers ESA in 1984; nowadays ESA McIntosh belongs to Havelock Europa of Dalgety Bay and makes only educational furniture.

LAUNDRIES AND TELEPHONE EXCHANGES

The growth of tourism in Scotland from the mid 19th century, and particularly the increasing number of hotels in St Andrews, no doubt contributed to the growth of two substantial laundries in Sinclairtown to keep available a fresh supply of bed and table linen,

up to 2,000 people; 'System X' exchanges were for a time their speciality. The plant lost its edge while supplying parts for Amstrad computers, being bought over and closed in 1991 by Hutchinson of Hong Kong; since then the building has been divided up and used by a variety of firms.

LIGHT INDUSTRY – LITERALLY

On the brighter side, Strand Electric – originally an offshoot of the London theatre industry as makers of theatre lighting – moved to Kirkcaldy in the 1960s as part of the Rank bakery and film empire. It has profited from the growth of television and a great demand for spectacular events, and with 300 workers in 1972 gained a worldwide niche in the making of studio lighting and the control of elaborate lighting displays. Bought out by its managers in the early 1990s, it has since earned fame by supplying the control system for the Sydney Olympics – over 3 million watts of lighting! There is no doubt that the town would benefit from more industries with such verve, but sadly few firms will nowadays venture so far north.

though a disastrous fire in 1990, competition and rationalisation spirited this activity away to localities nearer the centres of demand. A newer firm, however, flourishes on the Randolph Estate. Also vanished is GEC, persuaded by the Town Council in the 1960s to build a very large factory at Mitchelston to make telephone equipment, which employed

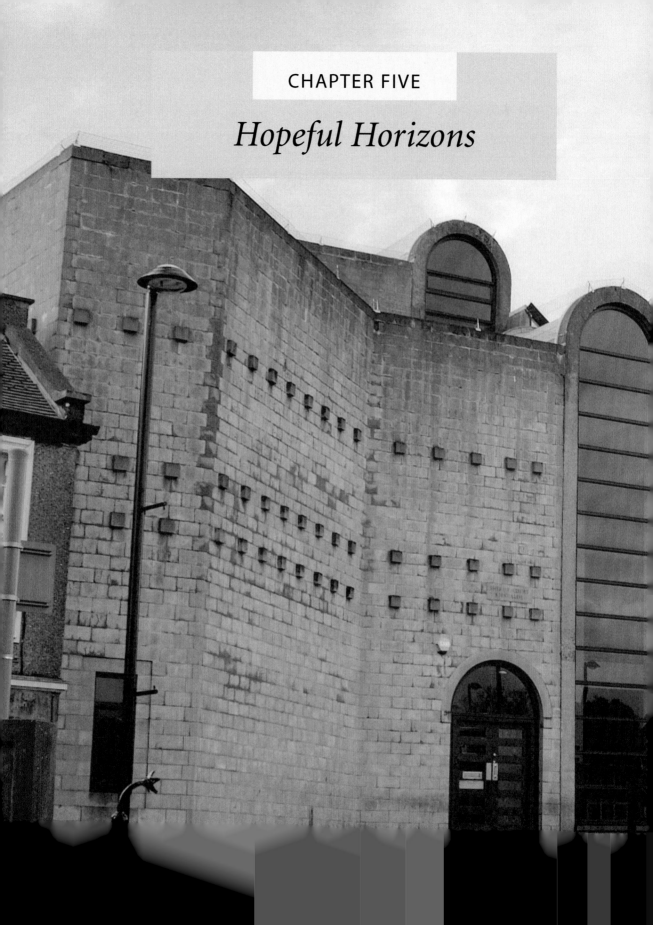

CHAPTER FIVE

Hopeful Horizons

A VIEW OF THE FIRTH OF FORTH COASTAL AREA AND RAVENSCRAIG CASTLE 2005 K197714k

KIRKCALDY and its neighbour Dysart share a magnificent coastal location, sheltered from northerly weather and with glorious views across the Firth of Forth to the occasionally snow-capped hills of East Lothian; to the east stand two prominent sentinels, the Bass Rock in its white cloak of guano and the conical Law of North Berwick, each an extinct volcano. Dysart, once the principal settlement, is now a part of the growing whole that is modern Kirkcaldy. It cannot be coincidental that such a remarkable locality has been the home of some of the world's most brilliant people, from the architect Robert Adam to the uniquely analytical Adam Smith, the vastly practical yet visionary Sandford Fleming, and the intrepid explorer McDouall Stuart.

Nowadays we can fly to the Australia that McDouall Stuart explored, or cross Canada on Sir Sandford Fleming's railway. Or we can stay locally and look east, beyond the frowning Ravenscraig Castle on its cliff overlooking the expanding town, to admire the sheltered coves and sweeping tree-girt green spaces of Ravenscraig Park. Almost alone among

DYSART, THE PAN HA', 2005 KI97715k

people living in municipal tall flats, those who are housed in Kirkcaldy's three fine Ravenscraig blocks are uniquely placed to enjoy these fine prospects. They may walk through the park to the belvedere overlooking picturesque Dysart harbour, recently cleared of nearly a century of silt and with its medieval stone breakwater soon to be restored. The old harbourmaster's house will soon become an interpretation centre

The Pan Ha', once home to the saltpans, was conserved with some rebuilding in the 1960s.

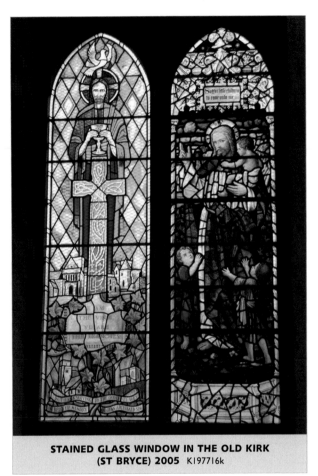

STAINED GLASS WINDOW IN THE OLD KIRK (ST BRYCE) 2005 K197716k

The left side commemorates the wife of John Sim, Minister here 1960–88; the right side is one of many windows donated by John Hunter of St Brycedale House.

for the Fife coastal path, which continues eastwards to the conservation villages of West and East Wemyss, and the Pictish caves beneath the wooded cliff-girt policies of Wemyss Castle.

Kirkcaldy may have passed through a bleak period, but it has magnificent parks, most of its old industrial debris has been cleared away, and the best of its many old buildings have either been conserved, or are in the course of strongly supported conservation efforts, as several illustrations show for instance K197715k, above left.

THE MERCHANT'S HOUSE 2005 K197717k

The recently restored Merchant's House, 16th century home of the Law family, stands almost opposite Kirkcaldy harbour on whose trade the family's evident prosperity was based.

THE MERCHANT'S HOUSE ZZZ03895

The Merchant's House before restoration, as Johnny Lena's fish and chip shop.

Farther afield, beyond the industrial towns and villages of Levenmouth, we may travel into the famed East Neuk of Fife, with its succession of characterful fishing villages, hotels and golf courses, and the sailing harbour of Elie. The East Neuk (or 'corner') climaxes in the prominent hill of Largo Law, the tiny historic port of Crail with its promontory of Fife Ness, and the ancient seaside, golfing and university city of St Andrews. Looking southwest from Kirkcaldy one can see the characteristic outlines of more volcanic features – Arthur's Seat and the Salisbury Crags – and on clear days Edinburgh Castle stands out, perched on its precipitous rock beneath the serried summits of the Pentland Hills, which stretch away in line, far into the western mists.

Inland, away to the west of the attractively wooded and well-used Beveridge Park, are ancient tower houses set in a tumble of green hills. These hills are crossed by minor roads giving astonishingly varied views, and culminate in the Binn above the historic town of Burntisland, which is separated from Kirkcaldy by an area of coastal sands surmounted by holiday developments and the picturesque village of Kinghorn. This, another ancient Royal Burgh, is perched on cliffs of hard igneous rock, which project into the Forth above Pettycur Bay and offer outstanding opportunities for observers of the busy seaway.

In 2004 the old Hunter Hospital, built in 1785 as St Brycedale House, gifted to the town by one of its many philanthropists John Hunter, was reopened by the Chancellor, Gordon Brown MP – whose father was minister of the adjacent church – after standing empty for 13 years. The hospital wings added in the 1930s were demolished, and replaced by two modern blocks, one of which is for frail elderly people. The house itself provides care facilities and meeting rooms.

Although the Orrock quarry and temporary opencast coal workings somewhat mar the less interesting landscapes farther inland, the new town of Glenrothes with its myriad trees and informal airport forms a foreground to the readily trampable twin summits of the Lomond Hills. From there walkers may overlook the fertile Howe of Fife, with the beautiful conservation village of Falkland – a gem of late medieval times – and farther still, hidden beyond the Ochil Hills lies Perth. On the distant skyline are the Grampians, reminding us of all the stark bens, hidden glens and manifold leisure opportunities of the Highlands.

HUNTER HOUSE 2005 K197718k

Hunter House – originally St Brycedale House and possibly a design by Robert Adam - was recently restored as the centrepiece of a development of social flats.

Travel between FIFE and EDINBURGH — by train

British Railways operate a regular half-hourly diesel train service between Edinburgh and the following stations:

Aberdour
Burntisland
Dunfermline
Inverkeithing
Kinghorn
Kirkcaldy
North Queensferry
Rosyth Halt

Over 40 trains on week-days in each direction. There is also a good train service on Sundays.

Note: North Queensferry Station and Rosyth Halt are closed on Sundays.

Ask your local Stationmaster or appointed Travel Agent for folder giving full train services.

SPECIAL CHEAP FARES
TO AND FROM EDINBURGH (WAVERLEY)

With	2nd Class Day Return	2nd Class Cheap Single
ABERDOUR	5/6	2/9
BURNTISLAND	6/9	3/6
DUNFERMLINE	5/6	2/9
INVERKEITHING	4/6	2/3
KINGHORN	6/9	3/6
KIRKCALDY	7/4	3/9
NORTH QUEENSFERRY	4/-	2/-
ROSYTH HALT	5/-	2/6

1st Class tickets also issued at approximately 50% over 2nd Class Fare.

The above fares are subject to alteration without further notice.

British Railways

BRITISH RAIL POSTER 1965 ZZZ03896

Thanks to inflation the day return fare to Edinburgh, then 7s 4d (37p), is now £6.20!

Regular trains from the modern station serve Edinburgh, Newcastle, York and London to the south, Dunfermline to the west and Dundee, Aberdeen, Perth and Inverness to the north. First Scotrail provides an intensive service of the latest diesel trains to Edinburgh, at best only 35 minutes away, which wind along the complex wooded coastline, offering rural glimpses, chance views of basking seals and the certain glories of Aberdour Castle, hiding its pleasant village resort. As they cross the famous Forth Bridge, now being thoroughly repainted after decades of sad neglect, passengers can glimpse panoramic views both east and west, from sunrise over the Bass Rock to sunsets behind the Ochil Hills and Ben Lomond. They may look down on vast oil tankers, speedy Continental ferries plying overnight to Zeebrugge, high-stacked container ships, and the occasional cruise liner or warship. Farther on is a grandstand view of Edinburgh's increasingly busy airport.

For the near future, the recently lengthened platforms on this line will enable longer trains to be put on at the ever busier peak

THE RAILWAY STATION 2005 K197719k

The striking modern railway station was opened in 1991, it replaced the 1964 fire-damaged building.

times, and although station parking remains an acute problem, there are plans to enlarge the station car parks by 400 more spaces. All that is lacking is the will, and some money!

Alternatively one may drive to Inverkeithing, park and ride into Edinburgh with a choice of train or bus, while a good network of express buses plies as far afield as Edinburgh, Glasgow and St Andrews. With good roads between Kirkcaldy and the Forth Road Bridge, albeit increasingly congested in the peaks, it is scarcely surprising that housing development in and around the

town has been continuous for half a century and more, providing an ever-widening choice to the prospective house purchaser. This ranges from Edwardian stone villas to the latest in large and luxurious detached houses, with new flats and unpretentious family homes aplenty, and not a few good quality former council houses for resale.

There has been a tendency in some quarters to denigrate our town centre, which has certainly suffered in the recent past from cuts in buying power, due to local industrial decline and an ageing population. But with

THE WALL PAINTING OF A GALLEON BEFORE RESTORATION 2005 ZZZ03897

This wall painting of a galleon was discovered during the restoration of the Merchant's House: was this the good ship 'Angel' – Scotland's best, chartered to collect James VI's royal bride Anne from Denmark?

all the big chain stores and many specialists represented in a compact area, seamlessly joined with two covered shopping malls, the fact that the ends of the High Street are not so prosperous must be accepted, just as motorists have to accept that they are unwelcome in its pedestrianised centre. This now hosts occasional Continental Markets, and in the Town Square is held the monthly Farmers' Market where fresh produce from Fife and other parts of central and eastern Scotland tempts discerning palates.

In the eastern area of the town, which developed largely independently of Kirkcaldy

A CONTINENTAL MARKET, HIGH STREET 2003 K197720k

This shows the first Continental Market, held in the High Street in October 2003. Holland & Barrett occupy the house where 'Pet Marjorie' Fleming lived 1803–11; it was refronted in 1923.

JOHN SMITH BUSINESS PARK 2005 K19772Ik

John Smith (1938–94) was leader of the Labour Party 1992–94; the John Smith Business Park was officially opened by his sister in 1997.

proper, Pathhead and Sinclairtown possess a wide range of specialist small shops, as well as the enormous and highly competitive household and garden store somewhat perversely named 'Rejects'. The northwestern area of the town, largely developed since 1945, boasts a modern retail park for use by those whose view of transportation begins and ends with the private car. Every supermarket chain is either available in one or other part of the town or is hoping to build a new store. Over the past decade MGt has developed a substantial call centre business near the A92 expressway at the northwest corner of the town, offering numerous jobs

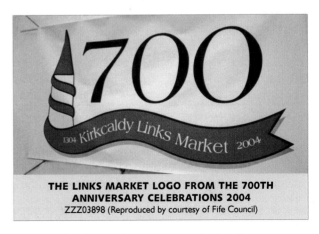

THE LINKS MARKET LOGO FROM THE 700TH ANNIVERSARY CELEBRATIONS 2004
ZZZ03898 (Reproduced by courtesy of Fife Council)

to people from the town and the former mining villages of central Fife; a second such building is nearing completion.

The Links area, once a mining community

on the shore to the south, gained its famed market rights in 1304; originally perhaps, rather like our own Farmers' Market, the annual Links Market – now in its eighth century – has evolved into Scotland's biggest fairground, with all the latest attractions that can possibly be transported around the country and set up for a week's frantic pleasuring. The 700-year celebrations included a huge marquee in the Town Square where many exhibits were on show and 'Medieval Methil' enacted a 14th-century lifestyle, including King Robert the Bruce creating Lords and Ladies!

The Town House, whose construction

THE TOWN HOUSE SQUARE 2005 KI97722k

The tartan paving of the Town House Square looks particularly striking in the rain!

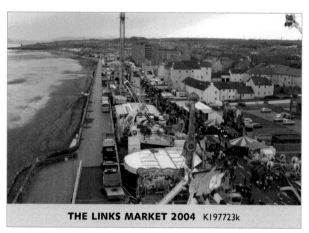

THE LINKS MARKET 2004 KI97723k

The Links Market in 2004, showing Kirkcaldy Sands on the left.

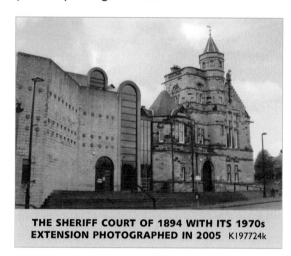

THE SHERIFF COURT OF 1894 WITH ITS 1970s EXTENSION PHOTOGRAPHED IN 2005 KI97724k

was set back by wartime and postwar delays, forms the centrepiece of the civic area. Its partial opening in 1953 was celebrated with a beer festival and many entertainments. Nearby is the listed Sheriff Court with its controversial extension, illustrated in the heading to Chapter 5 and above right, which deals with civic problems over a wide area.

The new Adam Smith College, largely rebuilt from Fife College in 2004, offers a wide range of courses, though the challenge is to keep our best educated young people from moving south, leaving an ageing population. Local health facilities for young and old are extensive, and have in recent years been upgraded with several new group practice surgeries, while the future of the Victoria Hospital as the principal trauma centre for Fife has been reasserted, and

THE OPENING OF FIFE COLLEGE 2004 KI97725k

The release of balloons marks the official opening of the new Fife College buildings in 2004.

secured by the seeing-off of a developer's attempt to build houses on the adjacent site where its future expansion is likely to occur.

We hope that we have shown you what an interesting place Kirkcaldy is, and how over the centuries it has constantly reinvented itself to face new challenges and accommodate itself to beneficial events. The regaining of the Scottish Parliament, which is already showing results in legislation framed to meet Scotland's peculiar needs, has brought renewed prosperity to Edinburgh and new housing pressures to Kirkcaldy. The Scottish capital is now so hard-pressed to provide enough housing that there has been a surge in the demand for homes in Fife, and particularly in Kirkcaldy, which now has such excellent train services to the capital that house prices have been rising exceptionally fast. The building of a large housing estate overlooking the Firth of Forth from the site of the former Seafield Colliery is in full swing, and equally large estates are rising in the north of the town on the old Chapel Farm. New flats are being built beside the harbour with its tidal dock, now used by the boating club. When these developments mature they will effectively complement the older areas.

In the interests of using brownfield sites and moving towards sustainable development, the Kingslaw area beside the railway north of Gallatown, currently undergoing opencasting, has been earmarked for future mixed development and hopefully a new station, once more serving the east part of the town. Kirkcaldy also needs a genuine train service to Glasgow, for the existing chancy change at Haymarket, supplemented by just one direct commuter train each weekday to and from Scotland's largest city, is laughably inadequate.

The possibility of a new ferry service across the Forth from either Kirkcaldy or possibly Burntisland to either Leith or Granton is being intensively studied. The harbour quays having – rather regretfully - gone for housing, the parking required for a ferry terminal would probably take the shape of a multistorey car stack at Pathhead Sands, beside the modern enclosed sewage treatment plant. Such a ferry, provided that it had really seaworthy vessels, would do something to relieve stresses on existing modes of transport to Edinburgh and the Lothians, and if it also carried cars, would open up new opportunities for shortened trips to England, and for the integration of tourism on either side of the Forth.

Some daring proposals have recently been submitted whereby the sweep of Kirkcaldy Bay would be interrupted by a rectangular projection, built out at vast cost from the Esplanade into the stormy sea in an exposed situation, bearing new shops – most likely a set of basic sheds containing cheap stores, at the mercy of rising sea levels and easterly gales bringing storm surges. Rather than so foolishly ignoring natural hazards and amenity considerations, the town centre should expand upwards when redeveloping, and also make better use of currently vacant upper floors over shops. The unique but controversial car stack at the Esplanade calls for the creation on its little used top floor of a restaurant with seaward outlook. In 1988 one Civic Society member proposed the laying out of a major new attraction in the form of a lengthy passenger-carrying miniature railway along the seafront, an idea that has recently been given some publicity, but an entrepreneurial flair is needed to make it a reality or to provide other missing amenities, of which a multiscreen cinema is the most obvious.

THE SAILOR'S WALK 2005 KI97726k

The restored Sailor's Walk with its 16th century painted ceilings will soon face new flats separating it from the harbour.

Looking to the long term, who can say what we shall face or how Kirkcaldy may respond? In antiquity, Horace sagely wrote 'quid sit futurum cras, fuge quaeere' – 'don't

THE ESPLANADE CAR PARK 2005 KI97727k

The unique Esplanade Car Park built in 1982 – a remarkable attempt to recreate tower house architecture!

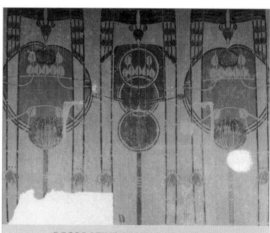

DECORATIVE PANELS IN DYSART PARISH CHURCH 2005 ZZZ03899
(Reproduced by courtesy of Dysart Parish Church)

These decorative panels in Dysart Parish Church (formerly St Serf's Free Church), were designed by the famous Glasgow architect Charles Rennie Mackintosh. Mackintosh painted these panels a century ago. They were only uncovered in 2005, and are now in the course of partial restoration, having been painted over many years ago by people who had no understanding of their value, causing much damage.

try to see into the future!'. More recently, Doris Day resignedly sang 'Que sera, sera' – 'whatever will be, will be'. Seeking advice from closer to home, and much as we may revere Robbie Burns, we cannot afford to be so downbeat as he was when he wrote '... I cast my eye on prospects drear, an forrit, tho I canna see, I guess and fear'.

As Burns foresaw, there will surely be political, economic and environmental problems ahead, but globalisation has opened our eyes to vast opportunities – and hitherto unimaginable threats. Perhaps those of us who dread global warming, and those who still deny it, should do something about staving it off, by cutting their wasteful use of energy, particularly in car commuting; those who may worry about the inevitability of asteroid impacts and super volcanoes must take heart from their rarity! Kirkcaldy people, like those worldwide, must be hopeful, brave, resolute – and above all, as a recent Channel 4 survey confirmed, keep always in mind that our best course is to treat others as we should wish them to treat us.

ACKNOWLEDGEMENTS

To Members of Kirkcaldy Civic Society who have assisted with writing this volume:
Sheila Goodfellow, Mary Hall, Anne McIntyre, David Potter, Robin Smith, Don Swanson, Ann Watters and Hazel Weierter.
Also to James Christie, Margaret Dunnett, Mary Frew, David Galloway, John Litster, Carol McNeill, David Reid, Katherine Shearer, Jocky Wilson.

BIBLIOGRAPHY

Kirkcaldy Remembered: Kirkcaldy Civic Society, published by Tempest Press
Kirkcaldy's Famous Folk 1, 2 and 3: Kirkcaldy Civic Society (3 books)
Kirkcaldy's Plaques: Kirkcaldy Civic Society
In the Steps of Adam Smith's Kirkcaldy: Kirkcaldy Civic Society
Missed Along the Way: Kirkcaldy Civic Society
Hunter House: Kirkcaldy Civic Society
Some Random, Rantin Rambling Rhymes...: Jock
The Making of Scotland: Robin Smith

17TH-CENTURY MOULDING 2005 ZZZ03900

This 17th-century plaster moulding of a cheerful angel adorns a ceiling in the newly restored Merchant's House.

Francis Frith
Pioneer Victorian Photographer

Francis Frith, founder of the world-famous photographic archive, was a complex and multi-talented man. A devout Quaker and a highly successful Victorian businessman, he was philosophical by nature and pioneering in outlook. By 1855 he had already established a wholesale grocery business in Liverpool, and sold it for the astonishing sum of £200,000, which is the equivalent today of over £15,000,000. Now in his thirties, and captivated by the new science of photography, Frith set out on a series of pioneering journeys up the Nile and to the Near East.

He was the first photographer to venture beyond the sixth cataract of the Nile. Africa was still the mysterious 'Dark Continent', and Stanley and Livingstone's historic meeting was a decade into the future. The conditions for picture taking confound belief. He laboured for hours in his wicker dark-room in the sweltering heat of the desert, while the volatile chemicals fizzed dangerously in their trays. Back in London he exhibited his photographs and was 'rapturously cheered' by members of the Royal Society. His reputation as a photographer was made overnight.

By the 1870s the railways had threaded their way across the country, and Bank Holidays and half-day Saturdays had been made obligatory by Act of Parliament. All of a sudden the working man and his family were able to enjoy days out, take holidays, and see a little more of the world.

With typical business acumen, Francis Frith foresaw that these new tourists would enjoy having souvenirs to commemorate their days out. For the next thirty years he travelled the country by train and by pony and trap, producing fine photographs of seaside resorts and beauty spots that were keenly bought by millions of Victorians. These prints were painstakingly pasted into family albums and pored over during the dark nights of winter, rekindling precious memories of summer excursions. Frith's studio was soon supplying retail shops all over the country, and by 1890 F Frith & Co had become the greatest specialist photographic publishing company in the world, with over 2,000 sales outlets, and pioneered the picture postcard.

Francis Frith had died in 1898 at his villa in Cannes, his great project still growing. By 1970 the archive he created contained over a third of a million pictures showing 7,000 British towns and villages.

Frith's legacy to us today is of immense significance and value, for the magnificent archive of evocative photographs he created provides a unique record of change in the cities, towns and villages throughout Britain over a century and more. Frith and his fellow studio photographers revisited locations many times down the years to update their views, compiling for us an enthralling and colourful pageant of British life and character.

We are fortunate that Frith was dedicated to recording the minutiae of everyday life. For it is this sheer wealth of visual data, the painstaking chronicle of changes in dress, transport, street layouts, buildings, housing and landscape that captivates us so much today, offering us a powerful link with the past and with the lives of our ancestors.

Computers have now made it possible for Frith's many thousands of images to be accessed almost instantly. The archive offers every one of us an opportunity to examine the places where we and our families have lived and worked down the years. Its images, depicting our shared past, are now bringing pleasure and enlightenment to millions around the world a century and more after his death. For further information visit: **www.francisfrith.com**

FRITH PRODUCTS & SERVICES

Francis Frith would doubtless be pleased to know that the pioneering publishing venture he started in 1860 still continues today. Over a hundred and forty years later, The Francis Frith Collection continues in the same innovative tradition and is now one of the foremost publishers of vintage photographs in the world. Some of the current activities include:

INTERIOR DECORATION

Today Frith's photographs can be seen framed and as giant wall murals in thousands of pubs, restaurants, hotels, banks, retail stores and other public buildings throughout the country. In every case they enhance the unique local atmosphere of the places they depict and provide reminders of gentler days in an increasingly busy and frenetic world.

PRODUCT PROMOTIONS

Frith products are used by many major companies to promote the sales of their own products or to reinforce their own history and heritage. Frith promotions have been used by Hovis bread, Courage beers, Scots Porage Oats, Colman's mustard, Cadbury's foods, Mellow Birds coffee, Dunhill pipe tobacco, Guinness, and Bulmer's Cider.

GENEALOGY AND FAMILY HISTORY

As the interest in family history and roots grows world-wide, more and more people are turning to Frith's photographs of Great Britain for images of the towns, villages and streets where their ancestors lived; and, of course, photographs of the churches and chapels where their ancestors were christened, married and buried are an essential part of every genealogy tree and family album.

FRITH PRODUCTS

All Frith photographs are available Framed or just as Mounted Prints and Posters (size 23 x 16 inches). These may be ordered from the address below. Other products available are - Address Books, Calendars, Jigsaws, Canvas Prints, Postcards and local and prestige books.

THE INTERNET

Already ninety thousand Frith photographs can be viewed and purchased on the internet through the Frith websites and a myriad of partner sites.

For more detailed information on Frith products, look at this site:
www.francisfrith.com

See the complete list of Frith Books at: www.francisfrith.com
This web site is regularly updated with the latest list of publications from The Francis Frith Collection. If you wish to buy books relating to another part of the country that your local bookshop does not stock, you may purchase on-line.

For further information, trade, or author enquiries please contact us at the address below:
The Francis Frith Collection, Unit 6, Oakley Business Park, Wylye Road, Dinton, Wiltshire SP3 5EU.
Tel: +44 (0)1722 716 376 Fax: +44 (0)1722 716 881 Email: sales@francisfrith.co.uk

See Frith products on the internet at www.francisfrith.com

FREE PRINT OF YOUR CHOICE
CHOOSE A PHOTOGRAPH FROM THIS BOOK
+ £3.80 POSTAGE

Mounted Print
Overall size 14 x 11 inches (355 x 280mm)

TO RECEIVE YOUR FREE PRINT

Choose any Frith photograph in this book

Simply complete the Voucher opposite and return it with your remittance for £3.50 (to cover postage and handling) and we will print the photograph of your choice in SEPIA (size 11 x 8 inches) and supply it in a cream mount ready to frame (overall size 14 x 11 inches).

Order additional Mounted Prints
at HALF PRICE - £12.00 each (normally £24.00)

If you would like to order more Frith prints from this book, possibly as gifts for friends and family, you can buy them at half price (with no additional postage costs).

Have your Mounted Prints framed

For an extra £20.00 per print you can have your mounted print(s) framed in an elegant polished wood and gilt moulding, overall size 16 x 13 inches (no additional postage required).

IMPORTANT!

❶ Please note: aerial photographs and photographs with a reference number starting with a "Z" are not Frith photographs and cannot be supplied under this offer.

❷ Offer valid for delivery to one UK address only.

❸ These special prices are only available if you use this form to order. You must use the ORIGINAL VOUCHER on this page (no copies permitted). We can only despatch to one UK address.

❹ This offer cannot be combined with any other offer.

As a customer your name & address will be stored by Frith but not sold or rented to third parties. Your data will be used for the purpose of this promotion only.

Send completed Voucher form to:

The Francis Frith Collection,
19 Kingsmead Business Park, Gillingham,
Dorset SP8 5FB

Voucher for **FREE** and Reduced Price *Frith Prints*

Please do not photocopy this voucher. Only the original is valid, so please fill it in, cut it out and return it to us with your order.

Picture ref no	Page no	Qty	Mounted @ £12.00	Framed + £20.00	Total Cost £
		1	Free of charge*	£	£
			£12.00	£	£
			£12.00	£	£
			£12.00	£	£
			£12.00	£	£
			£12.00	£	£

Please allow 28 days for delivery. Offer available to one UK address only

	* Post & handling	£3.80
	Total Order Cost	£

Title of this book . . . .

I enclose a cheque/postal order for £ . . . .
made payable to 'The Francis Frith Collection'

OR please debit my Mastercard / Visa / Maestro card, details below

Card Number:

Issue No (Maestro only):   Valid from (Maestro):

Card Security Number: Expires:

Signature:

Name Mr/Mrs/Ms . . . .

Address . . . .

. . . .

. . . .

. . . . Postcode . . . .

Daytime Tel No . . . .

Email . . . .

Valid to 31/12/16

Free Print – see overleaf

FF013554